Property
of
George F. Zimmerm

# THE
# SEARCH FOR
# HOLY LIVING

EDITED AND CONTEMPORIZED BY
## MARVIN D. HINTEN

BARBOUR
PUBLISHING, INC.
Uhrichsville, Ohio

© MCMXCIX by Barbour Publishing, Inc.

ISBN 1-57748-446-0

All Scripture quotations marked (KJV) are taken from the Authorized King James Version of the Bible.

All Scripture quotations marked (NIV) are taken from the HOLY BIBLE: NEW INTERNATIONAL VERSION®. NIV®. © 1973, 1978, 1984 by International Bible Society. Used by permission of Zondervan Publishing House. All rights reserved.

Unmarked Scripture quotations are the editor's paraphrases.

Published by Barbour Publishing, Inc., P.O. Box 719, Uhrichsville, Ohio 44683
http://www.barbourbooks.com

Member of the
Evangelical Christian
Publishers Association

Printed in the United States of America.

# CONTENTS

# INTRODUCTION

Ideas are timeless, but language is not. The most recent of the three authors featured in this collection is William Law, who wrote primarily in the 1720s. A few years later, the eighteenth-century author and critic Dr. Samuel Johnson called one of Law's works the "finest piece of hortatory theology in any language." But words like "hortatory" have passed from our vocabulary, and the nuggets of gold in seventeenth- and eighteenth-century books lie buried under centuries of language change.

Now the gold is again at the surface. This modernized and abridged edition provides the essence of four books published between 1600 and 1730: William Law's *A Serious Call to a Devout and Holy Life* (1729); William Law's *Christian Perfection* (1726); Jeremy Taylor's *The Rules and Exercises of Holy Living*, with a few additions from its companion volume, *Holy Dying* (1650); and Francis de Sales's *Introduction to the Devout Life* (1609). Essentially, I have attempted to distill the finest thoughts and phrases of these classic writers into a portable spiritual manual that you can return to again and again.

More specifically, what has been eliminated? Primarily three features. First, I have streamlined the ornate and elaborate repetition that was a hallmark of seventeenth- and eighteenth-century British style. (Law and Taylor are great offenders here—Francis, the French writer, is not.) A paragraph of flowery, overblown rhetoric may be delightful; a book of it is tedious.

Second, I have eliminated in this essence treatment thoughts that I believe are irrelevant and less helpful to today's reader. A critical scholarly edition of one of these classics would present everything just as the author wrote it. But a devotional edition can omit passages that seemingly possess less value. Notice the word "omit"; except for modernizing the language, I have not changed the essence of these writers' statements.

Before discussing the third feature eliminated, perhaps I should further comment on the types of changes made. I have freely modernized both the diction and the illustrations. (For

*Introduction to the Devout Life,* since it was originally written in seventeenth-century French, I used English translations from a century or so back for updating and abridging.) Where Law uses carriages, for example, I have used cars. In *Introduction,* I have also used cars in place of clocks, when Francis was talking about how people take their clocks in to the mechanics to get the oil changed! Other places you may be fooled into thinking examples have been changed where they haven't, as when Francis talks about tennis, a popular sport in seventeenth-century France.

But only the illustrations and diction are modernized; in condensing and restating the thoughts of Francis, Taylor, and Law, I have not substituted my own. Thus, when Law claims in this edition of *Serious Call* that girls might well outdo boys in science and public speaking if given the opportunity, I am not arbitrarily imposing twentieth-century feminism on his ideas. (The original says that if girls were allowed to compete with boys, in "arts and sciences, of learning and eloquence. . .I have much suspicion they would often prove our superiors.") Law was hardly a feminist in the modern sense. But as this example indicates, he was hardly a product of his times either, and I have tried to let each author's individual personality, interests, and ideas shine through.

The final feature eliminated is—and I am not quite sure how best to phrase this—the odd or humorous. Perhaps a couple of examples can help clarify. Francis loves analogies. He is, along with C. S. Lewis, one of the most analogical writers in the history of the church. Many of his analogies come from nature. Unfortunately, one of the main sources of biological knowledge in seventeenth-century France was a Roman writer named Pliny, whose information on the natural world today seems laughable. Francis uses Pliny repeatedly, and this leads to analogies that I feared would be distracting to modern readers, as when Francis asks us to drain away bitterness from our hearts just as (according to Pliny) draining the sap from the bottom of an almond tree makes its nuts sweeter. One of these nature-analogies I eliminated with great reluctance, partly because it is so "cute," and partly because C. S. Lewis and his brother Warren got such amusement from it. Francis asserts, again following Pliny, that we should take Communion as often as possible because taking elements of purity into ourselves will increase our own purity, just as rabbits become white in the wintertime because all they eat is snow! Although not true, one feels that it somehow should be.

The failures of Francis, Taylor, and Law may seem obvious to us, living in a different age; but our own failures would seem equally obvious to them. Each of their books emphasizes the need for radical behavior change; all of them would find odd the tendency of our time to proclaim, "Simply say a prayer and be saved—nothing else is necessary." "Let Jesus be your Savior now; later on you will also want to make Him your Lord." To the three authors included here, the idea of Jesus split into a Savior-part and a Lord-part, with people allowed to choose which portion they want, would be unthinkable.

And even a feature like Taylor's preoccupation with death can serve as a corrective to the contemporary church. Our lack of exposure to death leads us to feel comfortably at home in this world. (When was the last time you heard anyone sing the old gospel song, "I can't feel at home in this world anymore"?) A walk through the aisles of any religious bookstore reveals that the Christian community is feverishly attempting to feel at home in this world. An acquaintance of mine said a few years ago, "I don't just want pie in the sky; I want ham where I am!" This attitude gives rise to the entire spectrum of Christian self-indulgence, from fashion (one book lists the five kinds of coat hangers a Christian woman needs) to accumulation of wealth (another book lists Swiss banks where Christians should open accounts). The volume you now hold takes us back to a time when Christians were not primarily purchasers, but pilgrims; more likely indigent than indulgent; not a market, but a movement. As C. S. Lewis never tired of repeating, every age is shortsighted—but two ages are unlikely to be shortsighted in the same way. And since we cannot read the books of the future, we must read the books of the past. Thus I recommend this volume to those attempting to follow the Biblical injunction to "get wisdom; get understanding."

There may be elements in each of these writings with which you will disagree. But they will encourage you to take God seriously, to try to please Him. In chapter 3 of *Serious Call*, Law says, "We cannot offer to God the service of angels; we cannot obey Him as we could were we perfect; but fallen men *can* do their best."

May this book encourage you to do your best.
—Marvin D. Hinten

# A SERIOUS
# CALL TO
# A DEVOUT AND
# HOLY LIFE

WILLIAM LAW

# WILLIAM LAW (1686–1761)

William Law was born in England in 1686. After attending Emmanuel College, Cambridge, he was ordained as an Anglican clergyman in 1711 and continued at Cambridge with a fellowship. In 1716 he was forced to leave both the ministry and the university for refusing to take the oaths of allegiance to George I, the new king and head of the Church of England.

Edward Gibbon, grandfather of the author of *The Decline and Fall of the Roman Empire,* hired Law in 1723 as a tutor for his son. During that time, Law produced his two greatest works—*Christian Perfection* (1726) and *A Serious Call to a Devout and Holy Life* (1729).

In 1740 he left the Gibbon household and retired to King's Cliffe—his birthplace—where he had inherited a small property from his father. Law devoted himself to prayer and good works until his death in 1761.

# Chapter 1
*The Measure of Christian Life*

Devotion is neither public nor private prayer; all prayers are mere instances of devotion. True devotion signifies a life given to God. A devout person, therefore, is one who lives no longer to his own will or to the way of the world, but to the sole will of God—one who considers God in everything, serves God in everything, and does everything to His glory.

God alone is to be the measure of our prayers. In them we look wholly to Him. We are only to pray in ways and for things that are suitable to His glory.

As we make God the measure of our prayers, we should also make Him the measure of our lives. Thus any use of talents, time, or money that is not strictly according to God's will is a miserable failure. We fill our prayers with wisdom and holiness in order to fill our lives with the same. Thoughtless ways of life are as absurd as thoughtless prayers.

Since people seldom consider this, we often see a strange mixture in their lives. They are strict about attending Sunday worship, but when a church service is over, they are just like those who never come. In their ways of spending time and money—their cares and entertainments—

they are indistinguishable from the rest of the world.

Take Julius,* for example. Though he wouldn't dare to miss church, he lives the rest of his life by whim. Yet the whole tenor of Scripture opposes an idle, careless life as much as it stands against gluttony and drunkenness.

If a woman were to tell Julius that he could freely neglect church services, Julius would consider her unchristian. But if she were to say that he should enjoy himself exactly as others do, spending his time and money like others of his economic level, Julius would never suspect her of blasphemy and false teaching. If Julius were to read the New Testament from beginning to end, however, he would find this course of life condemned on every page.

We would doubt the spiritual depth of a person who claims to lead the Christian life without prayer. But to ignore our own use of time and money is as foolish as ignoring prayer. And to spend our lives in ways that we cannot (or do not) offer to God is as foolish as making up prayers without offering them to God.

Christianity prescribes guidelines to govern the ordinary actions of our lives. Thus to follow those guidelines is just as important as to worship God. Christianity teaches us how to eat and drink; how to use our time and money; how to behave toward the sick, poor, and old; whom to particularly love and esteem; how to treat our enemies; and how to deny ourselves. Each of these aspects of the faith is as important as worship.

The Gospels never prescribe public worship; it is perhaps the duty least insisted upon in Scripture. Frequent attendance at worship is nowhere commanded in all the New Testament. On the other hand, the devotion that

*All persons in *A Serious Call* are imaginary, invented by Law to illustrate his points.

14

should govern the ordinary actions of our lives is found in almost every verse of Scripture. Jesus and His apostles are wholly taken up in the doctrines that relate to the common life. They call us to reject the world and to differ in every way from its spirit; to reject the world's goods and to fear none of its evils; to live as pilgrims in spiritual watching, holy fear, and heavenly aspiration; and to take up our daily crosses, denying ourselves.

They teach us to seek blessed mourning and spiritual poverty; to forsake the vanity of riches; to not worry about the future; to live in profound humility; and to rejoice in worldly suffering.

Furthermore, we are to reject lust, greed, and pride; to forgive and bless our enemies; to love mankind as God does; to give up our whole hearts and affections to God; and to strive to enter through the narrow gate into a life of eternal glory.

This is what our blessed Savior taught as devotion. Isn't it strange, then, that people place so much emphasis upon attendance at public worship and so little on these daily duties commanded in every page of the Gospels?

If we are to hold to contempt for the world and affection for heaven, these things must appear consistently throughout our lives. If self-denial is a condition of salvation, all of us who would be saved must make it part of our everyday lives. If contentment and thankfulness are duties to God, they are duties in every circumstance. If we are to be new creatures in Christ, we must also demonstrate new ways of living.

Thus it is with all Christian virtues; they are not ours unless they are ours daily. Christianity does not allow us to live in the common manner, conforming to fads and indulging ourselves. We must live above and contrary to the world. If our lives are not daily courses of humility, self-denial, and heavenly affection, we are not living the Christian life.

But this concept is alien to most churchgoers. We see these people nicely dressed, singing hymns, and enjoying fine preachers in polite company. If we look into their lives, though, we see them to be the same sort of people as those who do not worship. The only differences between them are differences of taste or personality. Both have the same worldly cares, fears, and joys; they have the same life-styles and mind-set. In each we see the same fondness for nice housing and cars, the same vanity for attractive clothing, the same self-love and indulgence, the same fondness for entertainment, and the same trifling conversations.

I am not comparing these "good Christian people" with thieves or prostitutes, but the moral non-Christians. Consider two moral men. Leo is good-natured, generous, and truthful. In religious matters, however, he hardly knows the difference between a Christian and a Buddhist.

Hubert, on the other hand, was raised a Christian. He buys Christian books and records. He knows the "true meaning of Christmas" and honors all the big-name Christians. He doesn't drink or smoke, is honest and truthful, and speaks of religion as an important concern. Hubert has religion enough to be considered by the world (and by himself) as a Christian, while Leo is far from religion. But let us consider their relationship to the world. In that respect, we will find Hubert and Leo very much alike— seeking, using, and enjoying all that can be gotten in this world, and for the same reasons. We will find that prosperity, pleasure, success, and recognition are just as much the sources of happiness for Hubert as for Leo. But if Christianity has not changed a man's mind in relation to these things, what can we say it has done for him?

Jesus said, "Take no thought, saying, What shall we eat? or, What shall we drink? or, Wherewithal shall we be clothed? (For after all these things do the Gentiles seek)"

(Matt. 6:31–32 KJV). If to be thus concerned with necessary things shows we are not yet of a Christian spirit, surely to be like the world in our concern for pleasure indicates we are merely adding Christian devotion to a heathen life.

## Chapter 2
### *Good Intentions*

Why are the lives of many churchgoers so strangely contrary to the principles of Christianity? Simply because people do not have the intention to please God in all their actions.

It was this intention that made the early Christians such fine examples of piety. And if we stop and ask ourselves why we are not as holy as the early Christians were, our hearts will tell us it is not due to inability, but simply because we never really intended it. We observe Sunday worship because we intend to do so. When we intend to please God in our other actions, we will be able to do so.

Let a clergyman cultivate such intention, and he will converse as if he has been brought up by an apostle. He will no longer daydream about promotions and fame. He will no longer complain about having a small church or a small car.

Let a businessman have this intention, and it will make him a saint in his shop. His everyday business will be a course of wise actions made holy to God. He will consider not just what methods make him richest, but which will make his business most acceptable to God.

Again, let the wealthy man have this intention. He cannot now live as he fancies. He cannot live in idleness, indulgence, and pleasure, because these things cannot be turned into means of holiness. He will not ask whether God will forgive the vanity of his expenses and the careless consumption of his time, but he will seek to discover whether God is pleased with his life. He will not look at the lives of others to determine how he ought to spend his income, but will instead look into the Scriptures and take to heart every instruction for rich men.

With such an intention, the wealthy Christian will have nothing to do with expensive clothing, for the condemned rich man in the Gospel was clothed with fine linen. He will deny himself personal indulgences, for our blessed Savior says, "Woe unto you that are rich! for ye have received your consolation" (Luke 6:24 KJV).

You may argue that dressing nicely is your only weakness, so it doesn't really matter. But that is like a person saying, "Except for occasionally burglarizing homes, I lead a good life." To comfort themselves about their use of fine clothing and accessories, people often look for someone who carries the matter "too far." A woman who uses little makeup may condemn a woman who uses much, yet their motivations and attitudes about makeup may be the same.

How is it possible for a man who intends to please God financially to bury his money in finery? This is just as impossible as a person who intends to please God with his words, then meets other people with swearing and lying. All wasting and unreasonable spending are done deliberately.

I have chosen to explain the problem of unholy living by appealing to intention, for it makes the case so plain. It is easy for an employee to know whether he intends to please his employer in all his actions. Likewise, a Christian can certainly know if he intends to please God with his life.

Consider two people; one prays regularly and the other doesn't. The difference between them is not that one has the physical strength required to pray and the other doesn't. The difference is simply that one intends to please God by praying, and the other one doesn't.

One person throws away his time and money on useless diversions. Another person is careful of every hour and uses his money for charity. The difference is not that one has power over his time and money and the other doesn't; it is that one desires to please God, and the other one doesn't.

The problem of unholy living does not stem from the fact that we desire to use money and time wisely, but fail due to the weaknesses of human nature. The problem is that we do not intend to be as responsible and devout as we can.

I do not mean to suggest that human intention can take the place of divine grace. Nor do I mean to say that through pure intention we can make ourselves perfect. I am simply saying that lack of desire to please God causes irregularities that by grace we should have the power to avoid.

# Chapter 3
*Striving for Salvation*

In His goodness and mercy God forgives our weaknesses and lapses. We have no reason, however, to expect the same mercy for those sins we live in because we choose to.

For instance, perhaps you have made little progress in acquiring the most important Christian virtues. You shrug off this lack of progress as inevitable; after all, you say, everyone falls far short of perfection. But that is not the point. The question is not whether perfection can be attained, but whether you come as near to it as sincere intention and diligence can carry you. Only when you have carried out the Christian life with your best efforts may you justly hope that your imperfections will not be held against you.

The salvation of our souls is set forth in Scripture as a thing of diligence that is to be worked out with fear and trembling. We are told that "strait is the gate, and narrow is the way, which leadeth unto life, and few there be that find it" (Matt. 7:14 KJV). We are also told that "many are called, but few are chosen" (Matt. 22:14 KJV). And apparently many who have taken pains to obtain their salvation will miss it: "Strive to enter in at the strait gate: for many, I say unto you, will seek to enter in, and shall not be able" (Luke 13:24 KJV).

Christianity is a state of striving. Many will fall short of their salvation because they didn't care or take enough action.

Therefore, every Christian should examine his life by these teachings. They are plain marks of our condition. If salvation is given only to those who strive for it, it seems reasonable to me to consider whether we are indeed striving for it.

Suppose my religion is only a formal compliance with the accepted form of worship in my area. Suppose that it costs me no pain or trouble; it puts me under no restraints; I have no careful thoughts or sober reflections about it. Isn't it careless to think that I am striving to enter in at the narrow gate?

If I am spending my time and fortune primarily for pleasure, and am a stranger to prayer and self-denial, then how can it be said that I am working out my salvation in fear and trembling? If I seek worldly enjoyments as most people do, why should I think I am among the few who are walking the narrow path to heaven?

The Bible makes it plain that salvation corresponds with a sincere effort to obtain it. Imperfect people will be received as having pleased God—in spite of their defects —if they have done their utmost to try to please Him.

Of course, we cannot offer to God the service of angels; we cannot obey Him as we could were we perfect. But fallen men *can* do their best. If we stop short of our best, for all we know we may be stopping short of the mercy of God, for God has not promised mercy to the negligent.

These truths should not fill our minds with anxiety. Rather, they should excite us to zealously seek Christian perfection. The best way for anyone to know how much he ought to strive for holiness is to ask himself what will make him comfortable at the hour of death. Anyone who seriously asks himself this question will answer that at death he would wish to have been as holy as he possibly could.

Penitens was a prosperous businessman who died at age thirty-five. Shortly before his death, some neighbors visited him, and he said to them, "Friends, I know your thoughts. You think how sad it is to see such a prosperous young man dying. Had I visited any of you in this condition, I would have probably thought the same.

"But now my thoughts are considerably different from yours. It is not troubling to me now to think about dying young or before my business is fully established. In a few hours I will be buried; then I'll find myself either forever happy in God's favor or eternally separated from all peace. Can any words sufficiently express the littleness of everything else?

"We consider death as a miserable separation from the enjoyments of life. Yet what is there miserable or dreadful about death besides the consequences of it? When a man is dead, what matters to him except the state he is then in?

"Our friend, Larry, as you know, died while dressing for a party. Do you think he is now distressed that he didn't get to live until the party was over?

"If I am now going into the joys of God, do you think it grieves me that I do not have time to make a few more business deals? And if I am to join the lost souls, do you think I would be happier joining them as a wealthy old man?

"When you are as near death as I am, you will know that age, wealth, and status mean as little as whether the apartment in which you are dying is well-furnished. If I now owned a thousand worlds, I would exchange them all for one year of devotion and good works.

"You may be surprised to see me so full of remorse

when I have belonged to the church and lived free of scandal. But what a poor thing it is to say only that I have not committed murder or adultery. Yet that is all I can say of myself.

"In my business I have been prudent and methodical. I have studied books and gladly conversed with people of experience and judgment. Why didn't I bring these attributes to Christianity? Had I only my frailties and imperfections to lament at this time, I would lie here humbly trusting in the mercies of God. But how can I call a thorough neglect of religious improvement a frailty or imperfection?"

At this point Penitens was stopped by a convulsion. He never spoke again.

# Chapter 4
*Gainful Employment*

People will differ in their choices of employment, but offering up to God a pure heart as a daily sacrifice is the common business of all. Therefore the rich should not gratify themselves nor the poor vex themselves—all must turn their labor into continual spiritual service.

In order to make our employment an acceptable service to God, we must engage in it as if it were a work of charity or piety. "Whether therefore ye eat, or drink, or whatsoever ye do, do all to the glory of God" (1 Cor. 10:31 KJV). Our employment, then, must glorify God just as our prayers do. If a person pursues his business simply to raise his income and status, he is no longer serving God in his employment. Vain and earthly desires are no more allowable in our employment than in our prayers.

Most types of employment are acceptable for Christians. But they should not take up all of our strength, thoughts, and time. No human business is as great or important as spiritual development and nurture. After all, the Scriptures represent this life and the greatest things in it as vapors, dreams, and shadows.

A businessman may justly think it is God's will for him to support himself and others by selling things. But if his chief end in business is to grow rich and retire in luxury, his business loses its innocence. Such a person lives no more to the glory of God than a person who gambles to achieve the same end. In the same way charity and fine clothing seem to be quite different. But if a person is charitable for the same reason another person dresses well (in order to be noticed and admired), there is really no difference in the actions.

A greedy or ambitious businessman might say, to excuse himself, that his business dealings are acceptable because he only deals in lawful items. But a glutton could similarly excuse himself by saying he only eats lawful foods. A Christian is required not only to be honest, but to be of a Christian spirit in all things, and to make his life an exercise of repentance, humility, and heavenly affection. This includes his business life.

It is clear that a Christian should enter no further into business than he can offer to God as a reasonable service. For Christ has redeemed us only that we should live to the glory of God. Without this basic motivation, the most lawful employment becomes sinful.

A man is not considered honest because he is fair and just to some people or upon several occasions, but because honesty is the measure of all his dealings with everybody. Such is the case with humility. It must be the ruling habit of our minds, applying itself to business and to all our plans and actions, before it can truly be called a part of us.

Therefore we must be honest, humble, and devout not only in particular instances, but in every aspect of our lives, remaining steadfast even against opposition. The more we pay for any truth, the better the bargain. Our integrity becomes a pearl only when we have parted with all to keep it.

# Chapter 5
*Responsibility in Retirement*

Those who are comfortably retired or independently wealthy often have vast amounts of time and fortunes at their command. Their freedom lays on them a great responsibility to choose and do the best things. Much will be required of them, for much has been given them.

If you are in this state, without a boss to serve, serve your own soul. Nourish it with good works, give it peace in solitude, strengthen it with prayer, make it wise with reading, enlighten it with meditation, tender it with love, sweeten it with humility, humble it with penance, enliven it with psalms and hymns, and comfort it with frequent reflections upon future glory. Teach it to imitate those angels who, though they attend human events, "always behold the face of my Father which is in heaven" (Matt. 18:10 KJV).

Every person's circumstances are bestowed upon him by God. We must therefore use every situation for Him. When people spend a little time in prayer and then waste the rest, or give 10 percent of their money to church and then squander the rest, they have not considered the nature of Christianity. If it is desirable to be heavenly minded at church, then it is always desirable.

If someone would prove to me that we do not have to always live for God, I could prove to him that we do not have to live for God at all. A person who believes in part-time Christianity may as well believe in part-time intelligence. And when we consider that belief in Christianity perfects us, raises us to God, and exalts our best side, who would wish to ever be free of it?

Thus when we are seeking to understand how a Christian ought to live, we must look to the highest precepts of the New Testament, we must examine ourselves by the spirit of Christ, we must think how the wisest people in the world have lived, we must think what degree of holiness we would wish for when leaving the world.

I have not overstated the matter. In fact, I am just complying with Paul's advice where he says, "Whatsoever things are true, whatsoever things are honest, whatsoever things are just, whatsoever things are pure, whatsoever things are lovely, whatsoever things are of good report; if there be any virtue, and if there be any praise, think on these things" (Phil. 4:8 KJV).

# Chapter 6
*Spending Money*

Our money is just as much a gift from God as are our eyes or hands. We have no more right to squander it away than to put out our eyes or throw away our hands.

The way we use money reveals much about our character and priorities. If we waste it, we do not waste a trifle; we waste something that could be eyes to the blind, a husband to the widow, a father to the orphan. We waste that which could not only minister comfort to those in distress, but could also lay up treasure for us in heaven. So if we part foolishly with our money, we not only part with a way of comforting our fellow creatures but with a way of making ourselves eternally blessed.

Suppose a person has a stock of extra eyes and hands that he can give to anyone who lacks them. But instead of giving them to the blind and lame, he locks them up in a chest or plays with them like toys. Would we not consider him an inhuman wretch? Suppose that he is promised an eternal reward for giving away the eyes and hands, but instead he uses them to decorate his house. Would we not consider him completely insane?

Money can have much the same nature as hands and eyes. If we hoard money or waste it while the poor lack necessities, if we use it for extra clothing while some people have almost nothing to wear, aren't we near the cruelty of the person who decorated his home with hands and eyes? If we indulge ourselves in useless, expensive enjoyments rather than gaining an eternal reward for wise use of money, aren't we plagued with the insanity of the person who played with spare hands and eyes?

Buying unnecessary luxuries lowers us. Those superfluous things are like weights on our minds that make us less interested in raising our thoughts and affections to things above. Thus when we squander money we keep it from the poor to buy poison for ourselves.

> *"When the Son of man shall come in his glory, and all the holy angels with him, then shall he sit upon the throne of his glory: and before him shall be gathered all nations: and he shall separate them one from another, as a shepherd divideth his sheep from the goats: and he shall set the sheep on his right hand, but the goats on the left. Then shall the King say unto them on his right hand, Come, ye blessed of my Father, inherit the kingdom prepared for you from the foundation of the world: For I was an hungred, and ye gave me meat: I was thirsty, and ye gave me drink: I was a stranger and ye took me in: Naked, and ye clothed me: I was sick and ye visited me: I was in prison, and ye came unto me. Then shall the righteous answer him, saying, Lord, when saw we thee an hungred, and fed thee? or thirsty, and gave thee drink? When saw we thee a stranger, and took thee in? or naked, and clothed thee? Or when saw we thee sick, or in prison, and came unto thee? And the King shall answer and say unto them, Verily I say unto you, Inasmuch as ye have done it unto one of the least of these my brethren, ye have*

*done it unto me. Then shall he say also unto them
on the left hand, Depart from me, ye cursed, into
everlasting fire, prepared for the devil and his angels:
For I was an hungred, and ye gave me no meat: I
was thirsty, and ye gave me no drink: I was a
stranger, and ye took me not in: naked, and ye
clothed me not: sick, and in prison, and ye visited
me not. Then shall they also answer him, saying,
Lord, when saw we thee an hungred, or athirst, or
a stranger, or naked, or sick, or in prison, and did
not minister unto thee? Then shall he answer them,
saying, Verily I say unto you, Inasmuch as ye did it
not to one of the least of these, ye did it not to me.
And these shall go away into everlasting punishment: but the righteous into life eternal."*
—Matthew 25:31–46 KJV

I have quoted this passage at length because one would
hardly think most Christians had ever read it. What in
their lives demonstrates their belief that their salvation
depends on these works? Yet the necessity of good works
is asserted here in the strongest manner.

We must conclude from this passage that on the last
day people who neglect these good works will be placed on
the left hand and banished. There seems, therefore, no salvation apart from these good works. Yet who can be said
to have done these things? A person who once assisted a
prisoner or relieved the poor? That would be as absurd as
labeling a person "prayerful" who has said one prayer in
his life.

Our Savior said, "If [someone] trespass against thee
seven times in a day, and seven times in a day turn again
to thee, saying, I repent; thou shalt forgive him" (Luke
17:4 KJV). If, therefore, a man ceases to forgive his brother
because he has forgiven him already (or has forgiven

several others), he is breaking the law of Christ concerning forgiveness.

The rule of forgiving is also the rule of giving. We are not to cease from giving because we have often given to the same person or to others. We are as obliged to continue relieving them as when we did it the first time. If we are unable to give, of course, we are under no obligation. If we can only occasionally give, then we should give occasionally; if we regularly have money to give, we ought to give regularly.

# Chapter 7
*Casual Christianity*

MANY people live with the precepts of Christianity in their heads, but with something else in their hearts. Thus they live from year to year as mere admirers of piety.

Flavia is well off financially. She takes communion and attends church. When she hears a sermon on charity, she thinks it is a proper subject and one that people need to be reminded of. She doesn't apply it to herself, however, remembering that she gave just a few months ago.

As for people on welfare and unemployment, she knows they are all cheats and liars and will say anything to get relief. It would be a sin, she reasons, to encourage poor people in their evil ways. You would think Flavia had the tenderest conscience in the world if you could hear her talk on the danger of improper giving.

She has every attractive home furnishing and every modern appliance. She takes every opportunity for entertainment. Suppose Flavia lives ten more years. Of her thirty independent years, she will have spent fifteen in bed (she sleeps late, since no job forces her to get up). Of the remaining fifteen, fourteen or more will have been spent in eating, drinking, dressing, reading romances, watching television, listening to the stereo, and idly chatting with friends and neighbors.

I certainly won't take it upon myself to say that it's impossible for Flavia to be saved, but this much can be said: She has no scriptural grounds to think she is saved. For her whole life is in direct opposition to what the New Testament displays as evidence of a saved life.

If you would hear Flavia say she has lived like Anna the prophetess, who "served God with fastings and prayers night and day" (Luke 2:37 KJV), you would call her a liar. But is this a bigger lie than for her to claim she strove to enter in at the straight gate?

She might as well claim she had lived with Jesus while He was on earth. Yet she could have been humble, serious, devout, a lover of good books, prayerful, charitable, and meditative despite the handicap of a sizable fortune.

It is true that indulgence, idleness, and gossip are small faults when compared to the "great sins." But even these seemingly harmless trespasses become great sins when one considers they hinder a holy attitude.

# Chapter 8
*Wisely Used Money*

IF a person can bring any one part of his life under the control of Christianity, he has a better chance to subject the rest, for God has been introduced to his thoughts.

Now by subjection, I mean subjection to God. If a woman eats less simply to improve her figure, or stops drinking simply because she hates hangovers, she might gain control over those areas without becoming a better person. But when a person is moderate or regular in anything because of Christian self-denial—to present to God a more holy life—he possesses Christian control. Bringing one area of our lives under Christian control helps our entire subjection, because it brings God more often to our thoughts.

Suppose a person should decide that, instead of watching the news, he will spend that time praying or reading Christian books. It may seem unreasonable to expect a person to abstain from things that are admittedly not sinful. Nevertheless I feel whoever would try making such a minor change would find his mind set on higher things.

Miranda (Flavia's sister) is a reasonable Christian. She has but one reason for doing or not doing something, or for liking or not liking something, and that is the will of

God. She divides her money between herself and other people. She will not give a poor person money to use for entertainment. But neither will she spend her own money this way; Miranda thinks she should be as wise with resources as she expects a poor person to be. This is Miranda's spirit. This is how she uses the gifts of God—she is simply one of a number of people supported by her fortune, and she differs from the others only in the blessedness of giving.

Three words describe Miranda's attitude about dressing: she does it neatly, cleanly, and cheaply. She is never bored; her spare hours are opportunities to pray. She eats and drinks simply, so that every meal is an exercise in self-denial.

The New Testament is her daily study; she tests herself against the principles found there. When reading the Gospels or Epistles, she imagines she is actually listening to Jesus or the apostles speak. She receives their words as attentively as if they were speaking specifically to her.

Miranda is sometimes afraid she spends too much money on books, for she cannot resist buying practical books (by practical, naturally, she means books on holiness and the Christian life). But, of all human writings, the biographies of devout saints are her greatest delight. She searches them carefully, hoping to find some principle of holy living to make her own. In fact, Miranda's head and heart are so full of wisdom and holiness that she finds it difficult to talk about any other subject. If you are around Miranda while she is speaking, you almost cannot help becoming a wiser and better person.

Miranda assists not only people she knows personally, but strangers as well. "I was a stranger, and ye took me in" (Matt. 25:35 KJV), our Savior said. Who can imitate Christ, Miranda reasons, while only assisting friends and acquaintances?

"It may be," Miranda says, "that I will sometimes give to those who do not deserve it or who will not use my money wisely. But so what? Isn't that how divine goodness works? Doesn't God make His 'sun to rise on the evil and on the good' (Matt. 5:45 KJV)? Shouldn't we imitate our Father in heaven, who 'sendeth rain on the just and on the unjust' (Matt. 5:45 KJV)? Shall I withhold money or food from a person because he might not be good enough to deserve it? I beg God to deal with me not according to my merit, but according to His own great goodness. Shall I use a measure against someone else which I pray to God never to use against me?

"Where has Scripture made merit the measure of charity? On the contrary, the Bible says, 'If thine enemy hunger, feed him; if he thirst, give him drink' (Rom. 12:20 KJV). This plainly teaches that we are to be kind even to those who least deserve it. For if I am to do good even to my worst enemies, surely I should do good to people I don't know.

"You may say that relieving the poor encourages them to stay on relief. The same objection could be made against forgiving our enemies—that it encourages people to hurt us. The same thoughtless accusation could even be made against God's kindness—that by pouring His blessings on both the just and the unjust, the unjust people are encouraged in their wicked ways. And the same could be said against caring for the sick—that treated people will no longer strive for health. When the love of God has filled you with compassion, you will no longer make absurd objections like these.

"Whenever you turn down an opportunity to meet the needs of a poor, old, or sick Christian, ask yourself this question: 'Do I sincerely wish this person to be a fellow-heir of glory with me?' If you'll search your soul, you'll find you really don't. It's impossible to truly wish that person the happiness of heaven while disregarding his happiness here.

"For this reason," says Miranda, "I give to whomever I can. Our Savior has said that it is more blessed to give than to receive. Actually, then, we ought to look on the needy as our friends and benefactors. They will be our advocates with God on the day of judgment. They will help us to a far greater blessedness than we are giving them."

# Chapter 9
*True Worship and Thanksgiving*

WE glorify God with psalms and hymns of thanksgiving simply because we are to glorify Him in all possible ways. Verbal praises and thanksgiving, however, are not necessarily more holy in themselves than other acts.

Actions are often more significant than words. If God is to be worshipped with thanksgiving, then it's obviously higher praise to thank Him in the midst of every circumstance than only to thank Him in a set time at church. It is easy to worship God in church, setting aside a few Sunday hours. A greater measure of devotion is to worship Him in difficult areas, such as humility and self-denial. It is better to be holy than to have holy prayers. I do not mean to downplay the value of prayers; I mean only to point out that they are a slender part of devotion, when compared to a devout life.

To see this more clearly, imagine a person who never misses church. He praises God lustily in hymns and prayers. But throughout the week he is bored, restless, and irritable. Can his songs of thanksgiving on Sunday be considered true? It is ludicrous to combine bent knees with proud thoughts, heavenly petitions with earthly treasures, and brief prayers with extended entertainments.

The Son of God did not come from above to add an external form of worship to the various ways of life already in existence. He came down in human form to call mankind to a divine and heavenly life. He called us to radically change our own natures, to be born again of the Holy Spirit, to walk in the wisdom and light and love of God, to renounce the plausible ways of the world, and generally to become fit for an eternal, glorious enjoyment of God.

A single instance of the earthly or sensual in a Christian's life is a defiling spot; it ought to be washed out with tears of repentance. But a continuing habit of earthliness or sensuality is, in effect, a renouncement of our profession of faith.

# Chapter 10
*Joy*

Some people perhaps object that the rules for holy living restrain human life too much; that by considering God first in everything, we fill ourselves with anxiety. Further, some might argue that in depriving ourselves of so many seemingly innocent pleasures, we must be made perpetually downcast, bored, and gloomy.

I will answer those objections. These rules are intended not for a dull, anxious life, but for precisely the opposite. Instead of being anxious, we will become contented; we will exchange pursuit for fulfillment. Before taking on a holy life we cannot understand the solid enjoyments of a sound mind. In effect, our lower cravings have spoiled our taste for truly good things.

Imagine a person free from pride, envy, greed, lust, and other passions. Would not that person find real satisfaction? But take away one virtue from his life, replacing it with one vice, and by that degree his happiness will be reduced. All trouble and uneasiness comes from lacking something or other. Therefore, anything that increases our desires and supposed needs correspondingly increases our dissatisfaction.

God has sent us into the world with few physical

needs—primarily food, drink, and shelter. Even if a person owned half the world, he would still have no further physical needs. The world is quite capable of supplying those needs. One would think that this by itself—a world created to fill man's needs—would certainly satisfy and content most people. But our passions fill our lives with imaginary lackings. Pride, envy, and ambition create desires as though God had created us with a thousand needs that cannot be satisfied.

Ask any downcast person why he is troubled. Almost certainly he will turn out to be the author of his own torment.

Celia is a fine example of vexation. She has an illness. It upsets her greatly, for she sees others who deserve disease far more. She blames God for "unjustly" allowing illness to such a fine person as herself.

If we could only infuse Celia with Christian humility, she would need nothing else to become a marvelously happy person. She would be grateful to God for any moments of improvement He chooses to allow, and be satisfied with her regular condition.

It is not Christianity that makes life anxious or uncomfortable, but the lack of it.

Many people believe a moderate dose of Christianity—not an excessive amount—will fulfill our lives. They believe vaulting ambition to be bad, but moderate ambition good. One might as well say that excessive pain hurts, but moderate pain feels good.

Another possible objection to rules for holy living is that so many things in this world are good. Created by God, they should be used; but following strict guidelines limits our enjoyment of them.

Suppose a person without knowledge of our world is placed alone with bread, wine, gold dust, iron chains, and gravel. He has no ability through his senses to use those items properly. Being thirsty, he puts wine in his ear.

Hungry, he fills his mouth with gravel. Cold, he covers himself with chains. Tired, he sits on his bread. This person will vainly torment himself while he lives blinded with dust, choked with gravel, and burdened with chains.

Now suppose some benevolent being would come and instruct him in the proper use of those materials, warning him that other uses of those materials would be either profitless or harmful. Could anyone believe that those strict guidelines would make his life miserable?

In effect, Christianity teaches us how to properly use the world. It teaches us what is strictly right about food, drink, clothing, housing, employment, and other items. We learn to expect no more from them than they can properly provide.

The Scriptures tell us that although this world can satisfy physical needs, there is a much greater good prepared for mankind, reserved for us to enjoy when this short life is over. Christianity teaches that this state of glory awaits those who do not blind themselves with gold dust or eat gravel or load themselves with chains in their pain—in other words, those who use things rightly and reasonably.

If Christianity calls us to a life of prayer and watchfulness, it is only because we are surrounded by enemies and always in need of God's assistance. If we are to confess our sins, it is because such confessions relieve the mind and restore it to ease, just as weights taken off the shoulders relieve the body.

If prayer were not important, we would not be called to continue in it. When we consider that the other things we do are primarily or solely for the body, we should rejoice at prayer—it raises us above these poor concerns and opens our minds to heavenly things.

How ignorant people are to think that a life of strict devotion is dull and without comfort. It is plain that there is neither comfort nor joy to be found in anything else!

# Chapter 11
*The Measure of Happiness*

Felicia is wealthy, attractive, and typical of her set. Ten years ago her favorite pleasures were television, records, nice clothes, cards, and light conversation. Her current enjoyments are the same, and ten years from now one would still expect no change. Felicia has never known a pleasant day in her life without at least one of these pleasures being available.

This happiness has deafened her to Christianity; she has been too cheerful to consider something as dull as eternity. It is for fear of losing some of this happiness that she dares not meditate on true joy.

Geneva is a devout but impoverished and unattractive maid. Suppose some woman would say, "I would rather be Geneva than Felicia." I would say that woman understood Christianity. Unfortunately, however, most Christian women expect the happiness of both Felicia and Geneva. In effect, to cite a Scriptural parallel, they want to be the rich man on earth and the beggar Lazarus in heaven.

It is easy to ridicule someone who sits hours every day in front of a television, vegetating through life. It is more difficult for us to see the waste in someone who maintains interest in a variety of clubs, entertainments, and activities.

But think of it this way: a person who tries to quench his thirst by continually holding the same tarnished, empty cup to his lips is ignorant. But is it any less foolish for a person to hold a variety of empty golden cups to his lips? If all the world's activities are only so many empty cups, what does it matter which you take or how many you have?

Perhaps it is difficult for us to meditate on divine perfection or to contemplate the glories of heaven; after all, those are fairly advanced meditations. But anyone can contemplate the foolishness of pride or the uncertainty of life; these require no particular mental vigor. In fact, these meditations are taught us by almost everything we see and hear. This is the wisdom that life continually teaches us: There is no real happiness outside of Christianity.

# Chapter 12
*Misery of Life*

Jesus said, "Blessed are your eyes, for they see: and your ears, for they hear" (Matt. 13:16 KJV).

This verse teaches us two things. First, the dullness and heaviness of most people's minds regarding spiritual matters is so great that it can be compared to lacking eyes and ears. Second, God has so filled every life with arguments for godliness that people will certainly notice them if only they will properly use their eyes and ears.

What could be a greater motive to a Christian life than the fleetingness of earthly enjoyments? And who can help noticing this every day?

What greater call is there to look toward God than the pains, burdens, and vexations of life? And who does not feel this regularly?

What message from heaven could speak louder to us than the daily dying and departure of our fellow creatures? The great end of life is not left to be discovered by fine reasoning and deep reflections, but is pressed upon us in the plainest manner.

Let us simply intend to see and hear, and the whole world will become a book of wisdom. All disappointments and miseries will become as advice to us.

Imagine a man with tuberculosis or cancer. Suppose this man is wholly intent on doing everything in the spirit of Christianity, making wise use of his time, money, and abilities. He has no taste for gaudiness or extravagance, but seeks all his comfort in the hope of religion. We would certainly commend his prudence. We would say he has taken the right method to make himself as joyful as anyone can be in such a state.

On the other hand, if we should see the same person with trembling hands, short breath, and hollow eyes, intent upon business and bargaining as long as he can speak, and pleased by fine clothing when he can scarcely stand to be dressed, we would certainly condemn him as a foolish man.

It is easy to see the logic, wisdom, and happiness of a religious spirit in a cancer-stricken man. Pursuing the same line of thinking, however, we will easily see the same wisdom and happiness of being holy in every other state of life. For how soon everyone currently in good health will enter a state of weakness.

Some people believe that if they knew they only had one more year to live, they would stop worrying about reputation and finances; they would devote that year totally to God. At this moment, of course, any of us actually may have only one year left to live. But suppose someone has two years left to live. Couldn't he just as easily give two years to God as one?

If a person were told he only had five years left to live, he would realize this world was not a world for him. He would begin to prepare diligently for another world. Now who but a lunatic would assert that he knows he has even five years left?

It is said that a day to God is as a thousand years and a thousand years as a day because in His eternity, the passage of time is insignificant. We are created to be eternal, so it doesn't really matter whether our remaining time on earth is thirty years or thirty days.

Imagine three different types of rational beings. One type lives a week, another type lives a year, and the third a century. If these beings meet together and talk about time, they will have quite different understandings of it.

To make a true judgment of time, we must consider the true duration of our existence. If we are temporary beings, then a few years may justly be called a great deal; but if we are eternal beings, a few years are nothing. Most people believe their actions have temporary effects, several years at the very most. But when we come to truly believe that our actions have eternal repercussions, we will take each of them more seriously.

# Chapter 13
*How to Pray*

Prayer is the nearest approach to God and the highest enjoyment of Him we can experience in this life. When our hearts are full of God, sending up holy desires to the throne of grace, we can be no higher until death is swallowed up in glory.

On days when they do not have to work, some people spend the extra time in sleep rather than in prayer. This is a crime against Christianity. If we can rise at a certain hour for work, what does it say about our priorities that we cannot rise at that same hour for prayer?

If we consider devotion to be simply a certain amount of prayer time, we may perform it in spite of excess sleep. But if we consider it a state of the heart that desires the Spirit of God more than all other things, we will discover that prayer and self-indulgence cannot coexist. Self-denial is the soul of holiness. Whoever lacks even the self-denial to rise for prayer has no reason to think he has taken up his cross and is following Christ. What conquest has he had over himself, what trials is he prepared for, when he cannot rise for prayer at a time when the world rises for work?

As to the format for daily prayer, I think most Christians ought to use specific forms or patterns. Each person should begin with a set topic; then if he finds his heart in the midst of prayer breaking forth into higher devotion, he can follow those fervors. Private devotion should be under the direction of a form but not tied down to it.

Sometimes our hearts are so full of sorrow for our sins that we cannot confess them in any language but tears. Sometimes God's light shines so clearly upon us and we are so affected by His love and goodness that our hearts worship and adore in a language higher than words; we feel transported by devotion.

On the other hand, sometimes we are so sunk into our bodies that our hearts are much too low for our prayers; we utter thanks and praises to God, but our hearts have little or no share in them. Thus it is necessary to be prepared for either occasion—form for the dull times and flexibility for the vibrant times.

The first thing you should do in prayer is to shut your eyes and in silence place your soul in the presence of God. Separate yourself from all common thoughts and make your heart sensitive to the divine presence. (How poorly we perform our devotions when we are in a hurry. We are saying prayers rather than praying.)

As often as possible, pray in the same place. If you reserve a room (or part of a room) for God, it will affect your thoughts; you will more readily enter a spirit of prayer.

When you begin your prayers, consider the attributes of God. Use names for Him that express His wisdom and majesty. Names that express God's greatness raise our hearts into worship and adoration. Although prayer does not consist of fine phrases or studied expressions, words that speak highly of God raise the thoughts of the soul.

If you are asking Christ's spiritual assistance, remember His miracles. This will increase your faith in His power and goodness.

In reading Scripture and other Christian books, whenever you discover a passage that gives your heart a new motion toward God, you should try to give it a place in your prayers. In this way you will improve your prayers; you will be learning new ways of making your heart's desires known to God.

A good way to begin morning devotions is to offer all that you are and have to His service. Receive every day as a renewing of life; let your heart praise the glorious Creator. Feel free to add other thoughts as your emotions and circumstances move you; offering your circumstances to God sanctifies them.

Christians often seem bored, wondering about how to dispose of their time. They should give part of their time to prayer preparation, searching for helps to a devout spirit. If they would transcribe Scripture-prayers and gather praises and petitions from the psalms, they could pray more meaningfully. If they meditated on these thoughts habitually, they could pray more deeply.

Why do most people benefit so little from prayer? It is because they do not consider devotion something to be nursed and cherished. But it needs to be continually improved with care and diligent use of methods and helps. Of course, Spirit-filled prayer is a gift from God, not attainable through our own power. However, it is generally given to those who prepare themselves for the reception of it.

Merle is an intelligent businessman, organized and efficient. He faithfully reads the business dailies and weeklies, keeps careful financial records, and generally increases his knowledge each year. The only thing he has not improved is his prayer life. He still uses the same thought level (and even the same words) that his mother heard him use when he was a child.

Merle never does any job, even raking the grass, without considering how to do it more effectively. But he has never considered how improvable is the spirit of devotion, how many helps a wise Christian may call to his assistance, and how necessary it is that our prayer should be enlarged and varied to reflect our lives. If Merle sees a book on prayer, he passes it by just as he would a Dick-and-Jane reader; he assumes he sufficiently learned both to pray and to read as a child.

How pitiable is this man's conduct!

Or consider Kevin, a successful dentist. He thinks that by refusing to read any other Christian book except the Bible that he exalts the Bible's status.

It is very well, Kevin, to prefer the Bible to all other books. But if you will read only the Bible because it is the best, why do you not follow this practice in your dentistry? Why do you not limit yourself to a single drill—the best?

In dentistry, Kevin searches out tools for every possible situation. In prayer, however, he thinks one tool sufficient. Devotion is right understanding of God; right affection for God. All practices, then, that heighten our comprehension of God are means of devotion. They nourish and fix our affections on Him.

## Chapter 14
*Pray With Gratitude*

B egin your prayers with a psalm. I suggest that you not simply read the psalm, but chant or sing it. This will call your spirit to its proper duty and tune your soul to worship and adoration.

Psalms create a sense of delight in God. They awaken holy desires and teach you how to ask. They turn your heart into an altar.

In all states of mind, our inward emotions produce suitable outward actions. These outward actions then tend to increase the inward emotions. For example, just as anger produces angry words, angry words increase anger. Likewise, chanting or singing psalms (the outward action) increases delight in God (the inner emotion). Souls and bodies have a mutual power of acting on one another.

I encourage this practice because it develops thankfulness. There is no state of mind as holy and excellent as thankfulness to God. Consequently, nothing is more important than exercising and developing this mind-set.

A dull, complaining spirit—often characteristic of Christians—is of all attitudes the one most contrary to Christianity. It disowns the God it pretends to adore. To not adore God as infinitely good is, in effect, to disown Him.

For a person must believe that the world's events are guided by the care of a Being who is all love and goodness to His creatures. If a person does not believe this, he can hardly be said to believe in God. But if a person believes that everything that happens to him is for the best, then he cannot complain about wanting something better. A complaint is an accusation that God has failed to be sufficiently good. Thankfulness is an acknowledgment of His goodness.

The greatest saint is not the person who prays most, fasts most, or gives most to charity. It is the one who wills everything as God wills, who receives everything as an instance of God's goodness. All prayer, repentance, and meditation are simply ways of conforming our souls to God, of filling ourselves with thankfulness and praise for everything that comes from God.

The shortest, surest way to happiness is to thank and praise God for everything that happens. If you thank and praise God for whatever calamity, you turn it into a blessing.

Therefore, it is a good idea to sing praises to God during your prayers. Some might object that this is like making our prayers public, doing them to be heard by others. But the privacy of prayer is not destroyed by having witnesses—only by seeking witnesses. Remember the Scriptural example of Paul and Silas, who sang psalms of praise while in prison, with the other prisoners listening to them.

Psalms 34, 96, 103, 111, 146, and 147 particularly set forth the glory of God. You may choose instead to take the finest parts of several different psalms and piece them together. Do whatever is fitting for your own devotion.

# Chapter 15
*Pray For Humility*

Your devotional life is not evaluated simply on how often you pray. Yet imagine yourself placed somewhere in the air, a spectator of all that passes in the world. You observe, in one view, the prayers that all Christians offer to God each day. Some Christians are constantly calling upon God, inviting Him into their lives regularly. Others pray rarely, only at especially convenient times.

Now if you were to see this as God sees it, how do you think you would be affected by the sight? Could you really believe that those who pray haphazardly receive the same benefits from prayer as those who pray regularly? Which group of people do you think most readily perceives itself as servants or slaves of God?

Scripture exhorts frequent prayer almost as strongly as prayer at all. We can be sure that those who pray frequently are receiving the real blessings of prayer. Furthermore, frequent prayer is an effective way of adding virtue to your life. Suppose a materialistic man were to pray every day regarding his materialism. He would pray through temptations as they arose and ask God's assistance in rejecting them all. Eventually he would find his conscience so much awakened that he could no longer earnestly pray that way without changing his life.

If you are considering what virtue to begin praying for, I recommend humility. It may be the least intended virtue among Christians. And since every good thought or action lays us open to pride, a person advancing in other virtues may actually be receding in humility.

Humility does not mean having a lower opinion of ourselves than we deserve, but having a just sense of our weakness and sin. We are too weak of ourselves to do anything, even exist. It is solely the power of God which allows us to do anything, including moving toward Him. Thus pride is like theft; the proud take God's glory to themselves.

To develop personal humility during your meditations, simply examine your life. Suppose that all of your thoughts would suddenly be transparent to the world. If everyone knew what secret motivations corrupt even your most noble actions, you would no longer expect to be respected for goodness.

Think how shameful the nature of sin is, how great the atonement necessary to cleanse us of its guilt. Nothing less was required than the suffering and death of the Son of God. Is there room for pride while we partake in such a nature as this?

All of us love humility and hate pride—in other people.

Turn your eyes toward heaven and consider how different you are from the angels. They do not contemplate their perfections, but they all have the same joy. Consider how unreasonable it is for human sinners to bask in their positions of respect while the magnificent seraphim give honor to God alone. Let a person who is pleased with himself contemplate our blessed Lord nailed and stretched out upon a cross, comparing himself to that meek and crucified Savior.

# Chapter 16
*Our Crucifixion*

In striving for humility, we must consider ourselves learners. We have to learn something contrary to our former habits of mind. We must lay aside our own spirit of self-centeredness.

We are born in pride, which stems naturally from our self-love. This is one reason Christianity is so often represented as a new birth and a new spirit. Gospel history is the history of Christ's conquest over the spirit of the world. True Christians are those who, following the spirit of Christ, have lived contrary to the spirit of the world.

"If any man have not the Spirit of Christ, he is none of his" (Rom. 8:9 KJV). "Set your affection on things above, not on things on the earth. For ye are dead, and your life is hid with Christ in God" (Col. 3:2–3 KJV). This is the language of the whole New Testament; this is the mark of Christianity. We are to be dead (to the spirit of the world) and live a new life in the spirit of Jesus Christ. But in spite of the clarity of these doctrines, many Christians live and die slaves to the customs of the world.

Our conquest of the world is pictured in the crucifixion. Christianity implies an absolute conformity to the spirit Christ showed in His self-sacrifice on the cross.

It was this Christlike spirit that made Paul so passionately express himself in Galatians 6:14 (KJV): "God forbid that I should glory, save in the cross of our Lord Jesus Christ." But why did Paul glory "in the cross"? Is it because Christ had suffered in his place and excused him from suffering? Not at all. It was because his Christian profession of faith had called him to the honor of suffering with Christ, and of dying to the world under reproach, even as Christ did on the cross. Paul immediately adds, ". . .by [him] the world is crucified unto me, and I unto the world."

For that reason the cross of Christ was the glory of Christians in Paul's day. It didn't just show their willingness to acknowledge a crucified Master. It showed that they gloried in a religion that was completely dependent upon a doctrine of crucifixion. It called them to the same self-sacrifice, the same meekness and humility, the same patient bearing of reproach, and the same dying to this world's happiness that Christ showed on the cross.

To have a true idea of Christianity, we should not consider that Christ simply suffered in our places, but that His special merit makes our sufferings acceptable to God when joined with His. Without Christ's sacrifice, our self-sacrifices would not be fit for God. And the opposite is equally true: Unless we are crucified and risen with Christ, His crucifixion and resurrection profit us nothing.

The whole tenor of Scripture points out this connection between Christ and us: "If we suffer, we shall also reign with him (2 Tim. 2:12 KJV); "Our old man is crucified with him" (Rom. 6:6 KJV); "If we be dead with him, we shall also live with him" (2 Tim. 2:11 KJV); "If ye then be risen with Christ, seek those things which are above" (Col. 3:1 KJV). In all things, then, our lives are "hid with Christ in God" (Col. 3:3 KJV). Thus an individual's salvation obviously depends on his personal death and resurrection joined with Christ's.

Since the spirit of the world nailed our Lord to the cross, everyone who has the spirit of Christ—who opposes the world as He did—will be crucified one way or another. After all, Christianity still lives in the same world.

"Because ye are not of this world," our Lord said, "the world hateth you" (John 15:19 KJV). We are apt to lose the meaning of these words because we tend to think they were meant exclusively for the disciples. But Jesus did not add, as a way of consolation, that at some time the world would cease to hate His followers.

You may perhaps doubt the relevance of Christ's statement for us today, saying that the world (or at least the part where we live) has now become Christian. Surely, however, you would not claim that most people in "Christian" countries have the spirit of Christ. And the world's profession of Christianity makes it an even more dangerous enemy than before. The favors, riches, and enjoyments of the world have swayed far more Christians than its persecutions ever did. Since the world no longer seems an enemy, more Christians are content to be directed by it.

How many consciences are kept quiet simply because their sins are never condemned by the church? How many individuals ignore New Testament directives because the Christian world does? How many of us would have the audacity to live our lives so contrary to primitive Christianity if it were not that the other people in the church live the same way? There is nothing that a good Christian ought to guard against more constantly than the authority of the Christian world.

## Chapter 17
### Pride and Education

One would suppose that Christian elementary and secondary schools, Bible colleges, and seminaries would teach young people to begin their lives in a spirit of Christianity. But such is not the case. Pride is the primary motivating factor we try to awaken in children and young adults. We do everything we can to puff up their minds with a sense of their own abilities. We exhort them to everything from corrupt motives. We stir them to try to excel others and to shine in the eyes of the world.

We thrust these motives on them until they believe it dutiful to be proud of their accomplishments. And when we have taught them to seek distinction, then we promise the world they will "amount to something."

If young people are in seminary studying for the ministry, we set before them some eminent orator whose fine preaching has made him famous. We encourage them to desire this type of honor.

Of course, the same is true of young adults outside seminaries. If they seem interested in becoming lawyers, we encourage them by telling them how much money a lawyer makes.

And, after all this, we wonder why children and young

adults grow older so full of pride, ambition, and envy. But if we teach a child to thirst for applause, is it any wonder that he will continue to do so the rest of his life?

Some might object to my line of reason, and argue that we bring famous speakers into seminaries so the students can imitate their speaking techniques, not so students will be impressed with their credentials. I can only reply that I never hear this distinction stressed. Further, I think it difficult to separate the lecturer's speaking ability from his fame.

One might argue that we need the spur of glorification to make young people industrious. One could as easily argue that older adults need glorification to make them industrious. And that is, in fact, just what we have: a population of very industrious adults without humility.

As Christians, we can remove the desire to be on top, to beat the competition, and not have the young grow lazy. Can anyone imagine that children educated by Christ or the apostles would have been idle? On the contrary, Jesus performed countless worthy and glorious actions while displaying a profound humility.

How then should we teach our children to view education? A certain Christian's conversation with his son illustrates a healthy approach:

"Son, I love you. But you are under the care of a much greater Father than I, whose love is far greater than mine.

"First of all, then, worship and adore God; think of Him magnificently, speak of Him reverently, adore His power, continue in His service, and pray to Him constantly.

"Next to this, love your neighbor—all mankind—as affectionately as you love yourself. Think how God loves all, how merciful He is to them, how carefully He preserves them. Then strive to love the world's people as God does.

"Son, I'd like to give you some advice about school. If you enjoy outdoing your classmates, you will want to see them do things less well. This is not right. Be as glad to see wisdom and intelligence in other people, then, as in yourself. God is as pleased to see other people learn as to see you learn. 'It pleases God'—let this be your only motive for good work.

"I want you to learn history, not because I particularly want you to be a professional historian, but so that at proper times you may look into the history of past ages and learn the methods of God's providence. Reading the writings of the wise, you may fortify your mind with their sayings.

"Fill your heart with love for God and your neighbor. Go no deeper as a scholar than these loves will bear.

"Have no ambition conflicting with your personal purity and perfection. Live in such a way that you can be glad God is present everywhere, aware of all your actions. Don't desire to put down your equals, and don't grow bitter at those who try to get ahead of you. Your humility probably won't do others any good, but it certainly is a good thing for you.

"There is one person, though, with whom you are always in competition, one whom you should continually strive to exceed in excellence—yourself."

# Chapter 18
*Female Education*

A Christian orientation is as important for girls as for boys. Tragically, however, girls have not only been traditionally educated in pride, but usually in the silliest forms of it.

We seldom encourage them to compete with boys in the sciences and in public speaking (where I suspect they would often prove superior). Rather, we turn them over to the study of beauty and dress. Indeed, the whole world conspires to make them think of little else. Fathers, mothers, friends, and relatives all have the same well-meaning wishes for a girl: may she have a pretty face, a fine figure, and fashionable clothes.

I believe that a woman's first step to humility would be to forget whatever she has been taught to desire. Generally speaking, even good parents primarily recognize and compliment their daughters in nonspiritual areas.

Society's treatment of women is a particular tragedy because in most areas they have such a clear understanding of Christianity. Christian women regularly exceed Christian men in holiness.

It's often said that women are naturally vain. That's as unreasonable as saying that Jews are naturally stingy.

Expectations and conditioning generally make them a certain way, not their natures. Popular magazines, television shows, movies, and advertisements often picture women simply as painted dolls, as frivolous creatures made to gratify men's passions.

Whenever a woman is complimented on something for which men generally are not recognized, she should consider that she is being betrayed away from perfection. Friends to her vanity are not friends. Women should remember that they live for God, not others; their reasoning ability is as great as men's, and they have not only the right but the responsibility to seek wisdom as fervently as men should.

We often accuse women of being too ready to accept the first handsome, pleasant man to come along. It's no wonder that they should like in men what they have been taught to admire in themselves.

How then should young women be brought up? Evelyn furnishes an example. She has two daughters, but never looks at them simply in that way. They are her spiritual children, and she is their spiritual mother.

Evelyn teaches them to do all kinds of work, both domestic and mechanical. "I want you to always be of service to others, whether you are rich or poor," she says to them.

Since society pressures women to be primarily concerned with their bodies, Evelyn strives to counteract that attitude. "My children," she says, "I want you to know yourselves. Though you have bodies, you are more than that; you are spirits. You are made in God's image for eternity. Everything physical about you is like clothing—something to be used appropriately for a while, but which is wearing away.

"Always keep in mind these two beings inside you. Your permanent part desires purity; your temporary part inclines toward pleasure. You often feel this internal war, don't you? And you know by reasoning that the permanent part is clearly more important. But movies, television shows, commercials, and popular magazines would certainly not teach you this.

"Considering your bodies as residences, keep them pure and clean. Considering your bodies as servants, give them enough food, rest, and clothing to perform their duties.

"If you give your bodies more attention than this or your souls less, you are unwise. In fact, a person more intent on adorning her body than perfecting her soul is as foolish as a person who would prefer nice clothes to good health. In short, cultivate your mind more than your body.

"As to whether you get married or remain single, I do not worry about that, and neither should you. Never consider yourself simply a person to be admired and courted by men. Live for your own sake, for God.

"Regarding handicrafts, I have not taught you those skills simply for amusement, as an activity to while away the hours. When you were little I left you to little amusements, but now you know God and yourselves. You know the worth of employing yourselves for God. So turn your handiwork into gifts for others, particularly the less fortunate, and your skills will be changed from busywork to holy service.

"Love those people most who most turn you toward God.

"Though you intend to marry, yet do not until you find a man laboring toward the same perfections you are—someone who will be a friend to your virtues, someone whose constant example will benefit you.

"Strive to do praiseworthy things, but do nothing in order to be praised. Don't expect a reward from others for right living. And above all, don't be proud of your own virtues. As soon as people start living differently from the world, Satan points out to them how wonderful they are for doing so. He is quite content that people do a good work if they will only be proud of it.

"Never allow yourselves, therefore, to look down on those who do not possess as many Christian virtues as you. Force yourselves to love them, and pray to God for them. Let humility whisper that you would have lost those virtues if God had left you to your own strength and wisdom."

# Chapter 19
## Love and Intercessory Prayer

I have spoken earlier about prayers of gratitude and prayers for spiritual growth. Now I will speak of intercessory prayer—prayer for others. Our Lord recommended His love for us as a pattern of our love for each other. Since He continually makes intercession for us all, we ought to pray for each other.

Christ said, "A new commandment I give unto you, That ye love one another; as I have loved you" (John 13:34 KJV). It certainly wasn't a new commandment for people to love each other; this had clearly been taught in the law of Moses. But its newness lay in its imitation of a new example—we are to love one another as Christ has loved us.

There is nothing in us more acceptable to God than our love for others, our wishing and praying for their happiness. Nothing else makes us more like God, the very source of love. But love unites us to God only when it imitates the love God shows to His creatures.

God wills happiness to all beings, even though nothing can increase His own unbounded happiness. Therefore we must desire happiness for others even when it doesn't create any happiness for us.

God delights in His people becoming more perfect; therefore we should rejoice in it. God is willing to forgive everyone; we should be equally willing to forgive. And God has given us all an equally accessible source of happiness (Himself), so that we would have no reason to envy or despise one another. We cannot possibly rival one another in God's happiness. And as for temporal, material things, they are so foreign to our real happiness that they should be no occasion for spite.

Regarding intercessory prayer, our external acts of love are limited by time, money, and energy. We cannot contribute physical relief to more than a few people. But through prayer we have infinite power. God attributes to us the acts of love that we would perform if we could.

We cannot care for all the sick, relieve all the poor, or comfort all of those in distress. We can pray for them, however, and God will consider us their benefactors. We cannot care for every elderly Christian; but if we thank God for those who do, we will be received by God as a sharer in that ministry.

A man who lusts after a woman is considered an adulterer, even though he has only performed the act in his mind. A person who longingly prays blessings for those beyond his reach is therefore considered a benefactor, even though he has only helped them in his mind.

Just as the sins of the world made the Son of God become a compassionate offering for all mankind, so no one of Christ's spirit can be without compassion for sinners. There is no greater sign of our own perfecting than when we love those who are weak and defective. All sin, of course, is to be hated wherever it is; but we must set ourselves against sin as we do against sickness: by being compassionate toward the sick. All hatred of sin must fill the heart with sorrow toward the person miserably mired in it.

Some Christians often think that if they can't bear

being around horrid people, that proves their love of virtue. But if this had been the spirit of Jesus Christ, if He had hated sinners in this way, there would have been no redemption of the world. The higher our sense of virtue, the more we will want to rescue those without it.

Why do we love others? Because they are wise, holy, and virtuous? No, for often they are not. We love others to imitate and obey God. God loves us in order to make us good; this, then, must be the pattern of our love for others.

Perhaps you will ask, "How is it possible to love a bad man as much as a good man?" It happens in the same way it's possible to be truthful to a bad man. You do not determine how truthful you will be by how good the other person is, do you? You know that truth is founded in God's nature, not in people's merits. The same is true of love.

Perhaps you will further ask, "Aren't we supposed to esteem and honor good men?" Certainly! But esteem and honor are different from love. Love makes you want another's utmost happiness; esteem makes you desire to be like another.

Constantly consider how you love yourself as a measure of your love for others. You know how unpleasant it is to do something foolish or to have your weaknesses known. Therefore, if you enjoy telling about others' foolishness or exposing their weaknesses, or listening to their weaknesses and foolishness being exposed, you do not truly love them. On the contrary, those are acts of hate.

If, as Paul says, the lack of love is such a great shortcoming that it renders our greatest virtues as empty sounds, we desperately need to study the art of love. I therefore implore you to seek love regularly when you pray.

## Chapter 20
*Intercession and Mutual Support*

In his epistles, Paul tells churches and individual Christians that they are the constant subject of his prayers. He writes to the Philippians, "I thank my God upon every remembrance of you" (Phil. 1:3 KJV). To Timothy he writes, "I thank God. . .that without ceasing I have remembrance of thee in my prayers night and day" (2 Tim. 1:3 KJV). The ancient Christians did not cement their hearts with human interests but with mutual communication of spiritual blessings, with prayers and thanksgivings to God for each other. Christians used to astound the world with their love for one another.

Pray for others, then, as long and earnestly as you pray for yourself. You will find your heart growing generous, delighting in others' happiness instead of just your own. If you beg God to make someone eternally happy, you will want to see steps taken toward that on earth. It would be strange to ask God to make a sick person well but not to care whether he gets the necessary medicine.

Though we are to treat all Christians as brothers, we can live in the society of only a few; therefore, we should particularly intercede for those with whom we have contact. If you are kind in your prayers to those around you, it will be much easier to treat your neighbors kindly. Nothing can make us love a person more than praying for him. You will find it easy to forgive those whom you are asking God to forgive. These prayers teach Christians to consider each other as members of a spiritual family, fellow-heirs of future glory.

Oliver is the minister of a small congregation. He loves his people and prays for them as often as he prays for himself. He tries to know everyone's way of life and spiritual state so he can pray for them wisely.

When he first served the congregation, rudeness or cantankerousness on anyone's part would drive Oliver wild; now it raises in him a desire to pray. It is delightful to see how vigorously he instructs and how firmly yet tenderly he reproves; he has first prayed for those he instructs and reproves.

Oliver has been greatly affected by James 5:16 (KJV): "The effectual fervent prayer of a righteous man availeth much." He reads how God said of Job, "My servant Job shall pray for you: for him will I accept" (Job 42:8 KJV).

From these passages Oliver concludes that extra-holy people have extraordinary power with God. This makes Oliver even more studious of Christian perfection, not wishing to hinder his prayers.

Parents should make themselves intercessors for their children. I suppose most Christian parents ask God to "bless" their children in a general way; but I'm speaking of prayer for specific spiritual needs. It would cause parents to be very careful of everything they said or did, not wanting their example to hinder their prayers.

How can people most readily perfect their hearts? By interceding with God for those who irritate or frustrate them. Suppose that you have a misunderstanding with a friend, neighbor, or relative. If you will ask God to give them every blessing and happiness you can think of, you will have taken the speediest way of setting your heart back on its Christian course. Great resentments between friends often arise from minor incidents; mutual prayer relieves the ill temper.

Intercessory prayer can reveal our true feelings to us. Steven was a good Christian with one serious fault: He loved to hear and tell the defects of everyone in the church. When he visited, you generally heard him say how sorry he was that Mrs. X had certain failings, which he proceeded to describe. He related the most uncharitable stories so tenderly that most listeners felt he showed true Christian concern.

Once Steven told a friend of another person's weakness, a weakness too shameful to be mentioned in public. He ended by saying how glad he was that the information was not publicly known.

His friend replied, "Steven, you say you are glad, for this person's sake, that his weakness is not yet well-known. Go home, then, and pray to God for this man. Pray as earnestly as you would if you were the one hoping to save your reputation. Beg God to save him. Implore God to rescue him from those who are spreading his shame with secret stories. When you have fervently prayed this, then you may, if you wish, tell another friend what you have just told me."

Steven was greatly affected by this rebuke. From then till now he has constantly interceded, and it has changed his heart. Now Steven would no more tell a story to reveal someone's weakness than he would pray to God to harm that person.

# Chapter 21
*Self-Examination*

Self-examination is a most helpful type of prayer. Scripture says, "If we confess our sins, he is faithful and just to forgive us our sins, and to cleanse us from all unrighteousness" (1 John 1:9 KJV). This verse implies that if we ignore or hold back our sins, we cannot expect to be forgiven. And, obviously, a person cannot confess sins if he hasn't looked for them.

Perhaps you simply confess yourself a sinner in general and ask forgiveness for your sins in a lump sum. That is as unreasonable as telling a grocer you want nothing specific, just food in general.

What is confession supposed to do, after all? For one thing, it should make you ashamed of your sins. Surely remembering particular sins will bring about a greater sorrow than generalization. True confession should be truly useful.

For instance, suppose that one day you were to exaggerate during a conversation to make yourself look better. If you were to recall the transgression, condemn yourself before God, beg His pardon, and ask the assistance of His grace against that sin in the future, what could give you greater help against it? If you should commit that sin the next day and go through the process again, the emotional pain and remorse would make you even more desirous of perfection. In cases of repeated sin, we would certainly see ourselves humbled and eventually changed. But a formal, general confession has little or no effect on the mind.

To make prayerful examination even more beneficial, a person should most closely and regularly examine the areas in which he has traditionally had most difficulty. For example, a person who knows that he has trouble with anger should consider every thought, word, and action for evidence of this passion.

A person should also examine his regular routine. Does the way he works or eats glorify God? These examinations will give a person newness of mind, desire for perfection, and wisdom of spirit such as he has never had before.

Always try to remember how odious sin is to God. Sin is a greater blemish to the soul than any filth or disease is to the body.

How easily God can create beings, we learn from the first chapter of Genesis. How difficult it is for infinite mercy to forgive sins, we learn from the bloody sacrifices, the costly atonement, and human deaths. God made the world by speaking, but He redeemed it by great labor. Because of sin, the Son of God was forced to become man, undergo a painful life, and be nailed to a cross. The bloody sacrifices of the Jewish law represent God's displeasure at sin. And the world is still under the curse of sin, with famines, diseases, and tempests.

Consider all the sacrifices and sufferings, both of God and man, caused by sin. This will teach you with what sorrow you should purge yourself of it. To consider how thoroughly you should repent, imagine what level of repentance you would expect from the greatest sinner in the world.

The greatest saints of all ages have indeed condemned themselves as the greatest sinners, a position toward which such examination will move you. There are many things you know yourself to be guilty of that you cannot be sure about in others.

To properly sense your own sins, do not compare your life with other people's lives. You may indeed have less outward sin than they do. But to know your own guilt, consider your own advantages. You are educated, you have opportunities to read good books, you have known people whose lives served as fine examples. God may know people who have made less use of their advantages, but you cannot; you must know more of the benefits available to you than to others.

When you see how a certain person breaks God's laws, suppose you had been in his circumstances. You might have broken more!

# Chapter 22
*The Highest Wisdom*

I have explained devotion as both prayer and the consecrated life. One would think that Christians would naturally seek devotion. Experience, however, clearly shows
that nothing has to be more repeatedly pressed upon our
minds.

A person who practices devotion is master of the most
excellent knowledge. And what could be better than to
know the true worth of things?

If a person had eyes that could see beyond the stars
but could not see anything close enough to be of practical use to him, we would reckon his vision very bad. In
the same manner, if a person has a sharp wit and retentive
memory but doesn't understand his relationship to God,
he lacks useful understanding.

A man is considered a fool not because he lacks the five
senses, but because he doesn't understand the proportion-
ate worth of things. Undeniably, then, the person with a
low IQ who seeks God wholeheartedly is wise; and the
Ph.D. who ignores God is a fool.

The highest understanding is to rightly know our Creator. The wisest judgment is to live as if in His very presence.

A person should also have thought, word, and action
for evidence of this passion.

# CHRISTIAN PERFECTION

# WILLIAM LAW

# Chapter 1
## *The Nature of Christianity*

Perfection may seem to imply some state that not every-one needs to aspire after, a degree of holiness not practical for Christians. But by perfection I mean simply holy conduct in every condition of life.

I call it perfection for two reasons. First, I hope it fully represents the holiness and purity to which Christianity calls all of us. Second, it's an inviting title.

To rightly perform our duties and to have holy attitudes is not only the highest degree of Christian perfection; it is also the lowest the gospel allows. None of us, pastor or layman, can go higher; none of us can securely rest any lower.

To illustrate, let us consider one particular aspect of Christianity, our love for God. Christians are to love God with all their heart and all their strength. Who can go further than this? But who can aim lower—that is, who can be excused from fulfilling this command?

What is true for loving God is true of our other duties. The yearning after Christian perfection is necessary for all Christians. As there is but one faith and one baptism, there is but one holiness, a holiness which all should strive for.

Someone may object that not all people can be equally good, just as not all people can be equally wise. That's true in one sense and false in another. For instance, if we consider charity as giving money to the poor, all people cannot be equally charitable, since some have much more to give away than others. But if we consider charity to be a charitable frame of mind, all people may be equally charitable. The charitable frame of mind is an aspect of Christian perfection.

As to our performance of Christian duties, there may be a great difference. One person may engage in many business dealings and be honest in them all; another may be honest in his few dealings. If they both have honest minds, they are equally honest, though one is able to exhibit his honesty much more often.

A person cannot exercise martyrdom till he is brought to the stake. He cannot forgive his enemies till they have done him wrong. He cannot bear patiently with poverty and distress until they come upon him. So, obviously, some acts of virtue depend on outward circumstances. But any person may have a spirit equal to those circumstances if they occur. A person who has no one to forgive is not considered hard-hearted, and a person who has no wealth to give away is not considered uncharitable. We are not all in distress. So people can differ in instances of goodness and yet be equally good.

There may also be differences in action founded in our differing abilities. One person may be wiser than another and see more clearly into Christianity, practicing it more effectively, while another is not so wise, yet practices his Christianity as best he can. Goodness consists in being faithful to what we know. If a person is faithful to the knowledge God has given him, he is as good as someone faithful to greater light. We can hardly reconcile it with God's goodness for one man to have five talents and another only two unless we believe that God is as pleased with the right use of two talents as of five.

Everyone is called to goodness and perfection; no one has ever fully achieved it. In spite of His giving the command of perfection, God in His mercy admits to happiness people who have not been perfect. If God did not pardon our frailties and failures, even the best men could not be rewarded. But consider now: Does God's pardon of failure prove we are not called to perfection? Does God's forgiveness of defects in our goodness mean we are not called to be good? Surely not.

Someone might claim that people can be saved without trying for the perfection to which they were called. But though people will be admitted to heaven without reaching perfection, it does not follow that people will be admitted to heaven without *striving* for perfection. There is surely a great difference between falling short of perfection and stopping short of it.

You say you will be content with simply believing and being saved? That is foolish reasoning. God gives rewards; men don't take them. No one should say, "I will practice just so much Christianity, and then take my heavenly reward." The yearning for perfection should be present in everyone, and everyone should desire to use his abilities to the utmost.

God sees different abilities and weaknesses in each person, and in His goodness He shows mercy to different levels of holiness. I grant that some people with very little holiness may be accepted by God. But consider: Though weak holiness may be accepted by God, it cannot be chosen by us. We are not living a holy life if we *choose* to be weak. God may be merciful to small holiness because of pitiable circumstances. But when we choose small holiness, it becomes great unholiness. This book, then, is about our necessary efforts toward perfection, our striving for holiness.

## Chapter 2
*Who Are We?*

Who are we? Why are we placed on earth? These questions have been asked by wise men through the ages. Human misery and the impermanence of enjoyments make it difficult for wise men to discover the source of happiness.

God has satisfied our inquiries by revealing to the world His Son, Jesus Christ. This revealing has opened His great secrets; it has given us all the information necessary to calm our anxieties and lead us safely to happiness. All we must do is not exalt our own poor wisdom against God. We simply allow our eyes to be opened by Him who made them, and let our lives be conducted by Him in whom we live and move and have our being (Acts 17:28).

There is now light in the world, if we are willing to come out of the darkness. This light has acquainted us with God. It has added heaven to earth and eternity to time, giving us a peace that passes understanding.

The revealing of Jesus Christ acquaints us with these facts: We have a spirit within us, created after the divine image. This spirit is now in a corrupt condition, enslaved to fleshly thoughts within a body-tomb. Blinded with false notions of good and evil, our spirits do not remember the taste of true happiness.

Christ's revelation further teaches that our world is also disordered and cursed. It is not the Paradise God created, but the remains of a drowned world, full of sin and the marks of God's displeasure. It is a wilderness where dreams and shadows sometimes please, sometimes agitate, and sometimes torment our short, miserable lives. Devils reside here, promoting darkness and seeking whom they may devour.

Man's natural condition, then, is like a person sick from several diseases. Knowing neither his illnesses nor their cures, he is enclosed in a place where everything he sees or tastes continually inflames his diseases.

Christianity puts an end to this. The entire purpose of Christianity is to lead us from all thoughts of rest and satisfaction here, to deliver us from the slavery of our own natures and unite us to God, the fountain of all real good. It does not leave us to cast about for worldly happiness but prepares us for the enjoyment of a divine life.

"I am the way, the truth, and the life," says our blessed Savior. "No one comes to the Father except by Me" (John 14:6). Just as everything was first created by the Son of God, so are all things restored by the same person. Just as nothing could come into being without Christ, nothing can enter a state of happiness with God without Christ.

The price of our redemption both confounds our pride and relieves our misery. How fallen we must be from God to need so great a Redeemer! On the other hand, how precious we must be that so tremendous a means should be taken to restore us to God's favor.

All the teachings of the Gospel are founded on these two great truths: the corruption of human nature and its new birth in Christ Jesus. One explains all our misery; the other contains all our hope of happiness. On these doctrines the whole frame of Christianity is built. Christianity forbids only things that fasten us to sin and commands only those duties which lead us into the liberty of the children of God.

Our corrupt nature makes self-denial and bodily death necessary. Our new birth makes the sacraments and the reception of God's Spirit necessary.

To know our true condition we must search after a life that is hidden with Christ in God (Col. 3:3). We pity efforts at human greatness when we see a corpse lying in state. But if Christianity were to form our judgments, the life of a sensual person, though that person might be renowned, would cause us just as much pity. As the apostle said, one who lives in pleasure is dead while one lives (1 Tim. 5:6). Thus our lives must be more than enjoyment and pleasure, which are often the signs of living men and dead Christians. Therefore, to know what is good for us, we must look at nothing temporary. We might as well dig in the earth for wisdom as look at worldly enjoyments to find out what we want.

You will see every person in the world pursuing his imaginary happiness, but when you see this you are seeing the world asleep, chasing after dreams. If you wish, you may go to sleep. You may lie down and dream, for that is as happy as the world can make you. But it is like sleeping in a ship when you should be pumping out the water.

Suppose some being should try to please you by describing how fine a place to live the sun is. He describes its brightness and mineral riches and tells you it is a peaceful place. Would you not think it a sufficient answer to say, "I am not meant to live there"?

When your human nature is trying to please itself with worldly joys and desires, is it not an equally good answer to say to yourself, "I am not meant to stay here"? For what is the difference between happiness on the sun to which you can never go and earthly happiness from which you are to be eternally separated?

Consider the littleness of human honors. In the Book of Esther, the great king Xerxes asked Haman, his chief minister, "What shall be done for the man whom the king wishes to honor?"

Haman, imagining he was the man, answered, "Have royal robes brought for this man—robes that you yourself wear. Have a royal ornament put on your own horse. Then have one of your highest noblemen dress the man in these robes and lead him, mounted on the horse, through the city square. Have the noblemen announce as they go: 'See how the king rewards a man he wishes to honor'" (Esther 6:7–9).

Here you see the insignificance of worldly honor. An ambitious Haman cannot think of anything greater to ask. Every man can see the littleness of all rewards—except those which he is trying to get for himself.

We ridicule countries in which people bury shoes and money with the corpse to help it in the afterlife. Yet if we understood life truly, we could as easily ridicule our living efforts. We may buy finer houses, put on nicer clothes, eat out more often, get more entertainment, and these will help us to be finally happy as much as shoes will help a dead man walk.

You don't think yourself talked out of any real happiness when you are persuaded not to be as ambitious as Alexander the Great. Conversely, you should not think yourself drawn away from real happiness by being persuaded to be as contented as Jesus.

# Chapter 3
*New Birth*

Christianity is not just a school for teaching better morals or polishing our manners. It is deeper—it implies an entire change of life.

What does it mean to be "born of God"? According to John, "Whoever is a child of God does not continue to sin" (1 John 3:9). This doesn't mean that anyone born of God is flawless and cannot fall into sin. It means that whoever is born of God is possessed with the idea of avoiding sin; he labors to keep from it.

One might say of a miser that "he sure doesn't spend his money." This doesn't mean he *never* spends money, but that he labors against spending, and expenses are contrary to his intention. An expense troubles him, and he returns to saving with extra diligence. Similarly, a person born of God intends only purity and holiness; in that sense, he does not commit sin. We attempt to avoid sin as a miser avoids expense. We are not Christians unless we are born of God. We are not born of God unless we (in this sense) do not commit sins.

Also, whoever is born of God loves. Christ said, "Love your enemies and pray for those who persecute you, so that you may become sons of your Father in heaven"

(Matt. 5:44–45). There is perhaps no duty of Christianity more contrary to our natural selves. We cannot exercise this duty until we are entirely changed.

Our Savior said, "Whoever does not receive the Kingdom of God like a child will never enter it" (Luke 18:17). The change from infancy to adulthood is great; surely the change from adulthood to infancy is at least as great.

Infants have everything to learn; they must be taught by others what to hope for and fear. In this sense we are to become infants, being taught what to choose and what to avoid.

And if the new life is like birth, the old life is like death. Paul says, "For you have died, and your life is hidden with Christ in God" (Col. 3:3). Our old self dies when we become Christians. Paul says in another letter, "For surely you know that when we were baptized into union with Jesus Christ, we were baptized into His death. By our baptism, then, we were buried with Him and shared his death" (Rom. 6:3–4). So baptism is not just a rite through which we enter the church, but a consecration which presents us as an offering to God, just as Christ was offered at His death. Baptism does not make us Christians unless it brings us into death and consecrates us to God.

We are to copy Christ. The Savior purchased humanity with His blood, not to live in ease and enjoyment, but to drink of His cup, to be baptized with the baptism He underwent, and like Him to be perfected through suffering. Again Paul says, "All I want is to know Christ and to experience the power of His resurrection, to share in His sufferings and become like Him in His death" (Phil. 3:10). Redemption came by sacrifice, and the redeemed conform to it.

Many people are content with outward decency— moral behavior with an old heart. A person need not be a Christian, however, to be fair. A heathen can be temperate.

To make these virtues part of Christianity, we must have them proceed from a new heart. A Christian should be honest for the same reasons and with the same spirit that he takes Communion. Just as eating bread and drinking wine are of no spiritual use without the proper frame of mind, so our other religious duties are empty and meaningless unless our minds and hearts are renewed.

Some people, when becoming Christians, believe that living the Christian life means "doing what church people do." So a man notices church people don't smoke, and he stops smoking. Or a woman notices that church people attend worship services, so she attends. But Christianity is not practicing a particular virtue, or seeing how few vices we can manifest, but letting God control our attitudes.

People think they have sufficiently reformed if they are different in some particular way. But it is a mistake to be contented with ourselves because we are less vain or more kind than we used to be. Those who measure themselves by themselves are not wise (2 Cor. 10:12). Christ is the only standard by which we should measure ourselves.

Only spiritual rebirth assures salvation. As the Scripture says, "When anyone is joined to Christ, he is a new being" (2 Cor. 5:17). All other attainments are insignificant, as Christ showed: "When the Judgment Day comes, many will say to Me, 'Lord, Lord! In Your name we spoke God's message, by Your name we drove out demons and performed many miracles!' Then I will say to them, 'I never knew you' " (Matt. 7:22–23).

So let us examine our spirits, and not consider ourselves safe because we act respectable and belong to the "right" church. If not all those who prophesy in Christ's name belong to Him, surely not all those belong to Him who are merely baptized in His name.

# Chapter 4
*World, Flesh, and Devil*

Christianity ranks the world as an equal enemy with fleshly desires and the Devil. God indulged the Jews in worldly hopes and fears, giving them a land on this earth to possess. The Gospel is different: "My kingdom does not belong to this world," our Savior said (John 18:36).

Further, He said, "None of you can be My disciple unless he gives up everything he has" (Luke 14:33). Even the lawful concerns of this world can render us unfit for Christianity. Serious businessmen generally look down on idlers. But a person who centers his heart on being a successful businessman is as unattractive to God as any other self-gratifier. What difference does it make whether a man ignores God in an office or a casino?

Worldly cares are no more virtuous than worldly pleasures; Christ calls us from both. It is a mistake to give our hearts to either.

I will agree that nature makes some cares, such as making a living, necessary. The same is true of some pleasures —eating, drinking, rest. But Christianity must control both the cares and the pleasures.

Some say our Savior's teaching about forsaking everything relates only to the first Christians. I agree that Christianity finds different circumstances in different ages. But though the external state of the church changes, Christ's teaching about the internal state of Christians does not change.

The world may sometimes favor Christianity and other times persecute it. This makes no difference in the need for personal holiness. Such attributes as humility, longing for heaven, devotion, love, and renunciation of the world are always to be part of the Christian life.

So we must examine carefully to what the first Christians were called. If they were called to suffer at the hands of other people, that may (perhaps) not be our case. But if we find them called to suffer from themselves, in voluntary self-denial, we can hardly limit that calling to the first century. Why would the kingdom of heaven require heavenly affection and worldly disregard in the first century, but make no demands on our own time?

Let us see what Scripture requires of Christians regarding the world. Mark tells us, "As Jesus was starting on His way again, a man ran up, knelt before Him, and asked Him, 'Good Teacher, what must I do to receive eternal life?' 'Why do you call Me good?' Jesus asked him. 'No one is good except God alone. You know the commandments: "Do not commit murder; do not commit adultery; do not steal; do not accuse anyone falsely; do not cheat; respect your father and mother."' 'Teacher,' the man said, 'ever since I was young, I have obeyed all these commandments.' Jesus looked straight at him with love and said, 'You need only one thing. Go and sell all you have and give the money to the poor, and you will have riches in heaven; then come and follow Me'" (Mark 10:17–21).

In Matthew it is added, "If you want to be perfect, go and sell all you have and give the money to the poor" (Matt. 19:21). Some imagine that Christ's expression "if you want to be perfect" means some uncommon perfection, a goal not meant for every Christian. The young man's question, however, plainly shows what he is aiming at; he wants to inherit eternal life.

It seems plain, then, that Jesus' command was not meant to achieve some extraordinary height, but was a condition of being a Christian and securing eternal life. For Jesus goes on to say, "How hard it will be for rich people to enter the Kingdom of God" (Mark 10:23).

Obviously, what was expected of this young man is expected of all rich men. For how would it be difficult for them if they did not have to give up their money? If they could keep their money and still enter the kingdom, the difficulty vanishes. The disciples clearly understood the difficulty, for they asked, "Who then can be saved?" Jesus answered, "With God all things are possible," implying that it is possible for God to effect this great change in people's hearts.

Some people might still imagine this command ("sell all you have") to apply only to the rich young ruler, and not to all people of wealth. But observe this young man's virtue. He was so eager after eternal life that he *ran* to Jesus, and put the question to Him on his *knees,* and for these things the account says Jesus *loved* him.

Can it be imagined that Jesus would make salvation extrahard for one desiring it so? Would He impose especially hard terms on one who had already gained His love? Would Jesus hinder this young man's salvation for a reason that others might ignore? Would Jesus send him away sorrowful on terms that would be eased after his lifetime, in a later generation? Jesus did not give the command to show authority of demanding what He pleased, but to reveal an attitude necessary for Christianity.

If Jesus felt He was offering the rich young ruler a reasonable proposal, that proposal must be equally reasonable for us.

# Chapter 5
*Pearl-Seeking*

The kingdom of heaven," Jesus said, "is like this. A man is looking for fine pearls, and when he finds one that is unusually fine, he goes and sells everything he has, and buys that pearl" (Matt. 13:45–46). When Jesus calls the kingdom of God a fine, valuable pearl, I take Him to mean that a great deal is to be given for it. When He says the man sold all that he had to buy it, I take that to mean the pearl cannot be bought for less.

Modern people want much easier terms than those of our Savior's day. In proclaiming the kingdom, we often tell them they need not sell *all* for this pearl. And we too often say that after buying it they may go on seeking other pearls as they used to do and yet be members of the kingdom of God.

The peaceful, pleasurable enjoyment of wealth is continually condemned by our Savior. "How terrible for you who are full now; you will go hungry!" (Luke 6:25). This hardly sounds as though prosperity and plenty are approved enjoyments for Christians. "But how terrible for you who are rich now; you have had your easy life!" (Luke 6:24). Woe is not threatened only to those who have enriched themselves by evil means, but to all who have taken consolation in wealth.

Some say that the story of the rich young ruler simply means we must sell our goods when they interfere with our religion; until that takes place, we may peacefully enjoy them. (One might as well say we need not resist the Devil unless he interferes with our church attendance.) From where does this interpretation come? Jesus did not say, "You may someday find it necessary to sell." His command to the rich young man was "Go *now* and sell."

Does Jesus' command mean a person must literally sell everything and give it all to the poor to inherit eternal life? I understand Jesus to forbid self-indulgence from the estate. The rich young ruler should not use his wealth for ease (as the rich man in the parable of Lazarus did), but should offer it to God for the relief of others. Selling all is a specific way of expressing that general duty.

If Christ had told sinners they had to repent in sackcloth and ashes, I would take the sackcloth and ashes to be a specific way of expressing the general duty; though the particular circumstance of sackcloth and ashes might be omitted, yet the thing intended, humiliation and sorrow, was always to be performed to the same degree. When Jesus related the Good Samaritan's charity and told His hearer, "You go and do the same," the listener was not to wait for an opportunity of doing the exact same action. He was simply to do the same *type* of thing.

Likewise, a man need not literally sell all he has to obey Jesus' command to the ruler. But it is necessary to comply with the principle intended, disregard for wealth. He sufficiently parts with his money who parts with the self-enjoyment of it and uses it to support others who lack it. To literally sell one's estate is no more necessary for renunciation of wealth than sackcloth is always necessary for true repentance.

Many people prefer to believe the literal sense of selling all, for they can thereby consider themselves excused from doing so. But if they would consider that the thing required is disclaiming self-enjoyment of wealth, they would find themselves concerned.

I appeal to your imagination. Suppose you were to observe well-to-do Christians enjoying their money, creating continual sources of entertainment, living in the best neighborhoods. Then suppose you observed Jesus, with no place to lay His head. He promises a treasure in heaven to those who will give up all for His sake. He proclaims woe to the rich and full. Now judge reasonably from your imaginings. Would you suspect these well-to-do Christians to be followers of that Lord?

Suppose someone were to send up this prayer to God. "Lord, I, Your sinful creature, born again in Christ Jesus, beg You to give me more money than I need. Enable me to gratify myself and my family in the delights of entertainment, fine eating, and a fashionable neighborhood. Grant that as life goes on I may continually become better off financially. Help me to perceive the surest ways of growing richer. This I humbly and fervently beg in Jesus' name. Amen."

The same attitude that makes an unchristian prayer makes an unchristian life. The way we live is our real prayer, for as Christ said, "For your heart will always be where your riches are" (Matt. 6:21). Our heart continually prays what our life acts. We would condemn a person who prayed a prayer like that, but would call Christian the life that matches it. There is perhaps no better way of judging our affections than to see whether we can in our prayers ask God to bless our main desires.

# Chapter 6
*Rich Man, Poor Man*

Does anyone think he is entitled to more pleasure for being wealthy? One might as well say a poor person, because he lacks certain possessions, is entitled to be a thief.

Why aren't poor Christians allowed to be impatient or complaining? Isn't it because Christianity requires the same virtues in every condition? Isn't it because Christ can satisfy us in every condition?

But the same reason could be given against self-indulgence by those who can afford it. A rich man who uses his money for pleasure is like a poor man who spends his time complaining. If Jesus Christ can make us rejoice in tribulation and be thankful in hardship, surely He can help us forbear luxury.

Some people say that wealth and poverty are neutral states in themselves; they are made good or evil by the inward attitudes of the ones in those states. This belief overlooks the fact that rich people *choose* to be rich. Thus their outward position reflects their inward desires. (I will admit that a poor person might be greedy. But he has not *chosen* poverty.)

So to say that a person who chooses to live in wealth

has a "treasure in heaven" attitude inwardly is like saying a person who constantly fights has a peaceable attitude inside. One might as well say the town drunk has a good inner attitude toward soberness.

Christians are to love God with all our hearts, with all our souls, and with all our minds. A person who has his heart and head taken up with worldly concerns can no more love God with all his heart and mind than a person with his eyes on the ground could look straight up to heaven.

To love God wholeheartedly, we must be convinced that our only happiness is in Him alone. We cannot believe this until we renounce all other efforts at happiness. If we look to God to supply half our happiness, we can only love Him with half our hearts.

One might say that wholehearted love for God is impossible. Even should we grant this to be so, we must not therefore stop the effort, but imitate heavenly love as far as human nature allows.

To defend a lack of affection for God, people sometimes claim that we cannot control our emotions. Some people who love God will, because of their background or nature, not feel as close to Him.

This is partly true. Our emotions are indeed influenced by our natures. But differences in our natures cannot justify a lack of desire for God. Two gluttons, by their natures, may approach and eat a batch of cookies differently. The ill-mannered one may stuff his face, while the well-mannered one eats one at a time. But desire for cookies is the controlling thought in each of them. One person may, because of his nature, be less emotional toward God than another; but the same desire rules them both.

All people desire what they believe will make them happy. If a person is not full of desire for God, we can only conclude that he is engaged with another happiness.

It's hard to love God wholeheartedly; we all know that. So why do we not remove as many hindrances as possible?

The person who recognizes that the world will not make him happy will find his heart at liberty to aspire after God. He will understand what the psalmist means: "I thirst for You, the living God. When can I go and worship in Your presence?" (Ps. 42:2). Until we have that desire, we are acting Christianity without feeling it, just as a stage actor makes an angry speech without feeling angry himself.

If our hopes for happiness depend on other people, our attitudes will depend on them. We will love and hate other people to the degree that they hinder or help our happiness. We can never act otherwise until we are governed by a happiness which others can neither cause nor prevent. When we live in this state, we will not find it troublesome to love our neighbors as ourselves. It will be no harder than wishing them enjoyment of the same air and sunlight we enjoy.

Almost all Christians place some hope of happiness in the world. We need not go to evil people; let us visit any good religious family, and we will find kowtowing and coldnesses and cutting remarks, all founded on worldly reasons.

These proceed from the typical Christian attitude. Busily looking after our earthly interests, we intend only to keep clear of dishonesty and scandal. This is using the world as a virtuous pagan does, and it develops good pagan attitudes. But not just cheating and lawbreaking are harmful. The bare desire for worldly things—and placing happiness in them—lays the foundation for unchristian attitudes.

Why do most people find it so easy to love and forgive a person on his deathbed? Isn't it because all reason for dislike or hurt feelings ceases then? All worldly interests being at an end, worldly attitudes die with them. This shows us it is necessary to die to the world if we are to live and love as Christians.

Some people think dying to the world means we must enter a monastery; but this is no more true than avoiding vanity in dress means to stop wearing clothes. We can eat reasonably, we can drink reasonably, and we can use the world reasonably. We may work, we may buy and sell, we may provide for our families—*if* we do those things within the bounds of necessity.

Some people excuse their excessive labor as family provision, saying they want to express love by leaving their children an inheritance. So, you love your children and want to see them rich. Jesus loved the rich young ruler and told him to sell all. We have Jesus' express command to love one another as he has loved us. Are you following this love when you leave to your children what Jesus commanded his beloved friend to give away to the poor? If you really love your children, you will teach them that heavenly affection is the only hope for happiness.

# Chapter 7
## *Suffering*

THE foundation of Christianity is that humanity was restored by Jesus Christ's death on the cross. As Christ was holy and accepted suffering, we ought to conform to His holiness and acceptance of suffering. Christ was sinless; we should flee sin. Christ suffered; we should be ready to face suffering.

If Christ had lacked either holiness or suffering, His sacrifice would have been incomplete. We cannot expect God to accept suffering without holiness; it seems reasonable there will be no holiness without suffering.

Some people might believe that we will not need to undergo suffering, since Christ's atonement took care of the suffering our sin inevitably results in. We do not, it is true, suffer to make His sacrifice more complete or add further value to His atonement. However, it would be foolish to think that since Christ is our righteousness, we need not try to be righteous ourselves. Similarly, His suffering for our sin does not mean we will not suffer ourselves.

It's plain that Christ's suffering has not removed all other suffering for sin. Surely death is a suffering for sin—and all Christians undergo death.

Christ's suffering took place on the cross. Our suffering

takes place on our own crosses in the form of self-denial. As Jesus said, "If anyone wants to come with me, he must forget himself, carry his cross, and follow me. For whoever wants to save his own life will lose it; but whoever loses his life for my sake will find it" (Matt. 16:24–25).

We are very careful to observe baptism because our Savior instituted it. We should be equally careful to observe self-denial.

We deny ourselves to keep from being tempted by a life of ease and comfort. Therefore we can engage only in pleasures that do not make us comfortable with temptation.

Christ said, "Happy are those who mourn; God will comfort them" (Matt. 5:4). This clearly refers not to mourning about a particular circumstance, but to a state of godly sorrow. One property of mourning is absence from entertainment. When a person begins to relish diversions and amusements again, we sense the period of mourning is near an end.

Most Christians agree that Christianity includes self-denial. But we understand self-denial in such a loose, general way that we fail to apply it to our lives.

Consider this instance from the Sermon on the Mount. "You have heard that it was said, 'An eye for an eye and a tooth for a tooth.' But now I tell you: do not take revenge on someone who wrongs you. If someone slaps you on the right cheek, let him slap your left cheek too. And if someone takes you to court to sue you for your shirt, let him have your coat as well. And if one of the occupation troops forces you to carry his pack one mile, carry it two miles" (Matt. 5:38–41).

We are to deny ourselves by exposing our cheek and suffering pain, pain which we could prevent by resistance. We are to deny ourselves by not defending ourselves in lawsuits. We must take up the cross of one injury after another, rather than contending at a trial. (Instead of securing our shirts in the lawsuit, we expose our coats to loss as well.) Anyone who would argue that we need not really accept injustice must argue that we need not really love our enemies, Christ's next command.

Some people claim Christ meant only that we are not to prosecute others. But this text does not concern a spiteful prosecution; it forbids a seemingly reasonable defensive lawsuit. Malice per se was already forbidden to the Jews of Jesus' day; but we are to go so far as to deny ourselves self-defense and justice. Many Christians think we may defend our rights if the law will support us. But Christian standards of meekness are not to be formed by human laws any more than our devotion to God is to be formed by human standards.

By personal power or legal contention we could perhaps repel injuries. But by defending ourselves, we raise our passions and embitter our tempers.

Meekness and self-denial suit the spirit of Christianity. Christians are to have forsaken all, to be dead to the world, to be as meek and lowly as Jesus. Pride, self-love, and human wisdom argue against such meekness and self-denial. But let all Christians remember what Jesus said at the close of His words on self-denial: "If a person is ashamed of me and of My teaching in this godless and wicked day, then the Son of Man will be ashamed of him when He comes in the glory of His Father with the holy angels" (Mark 8:38).

People may pretend what they please about an "inner love" while they are resisting harm or engaging in lawsuits. But Christian love is to be like the love of Christ, who died for His enemies. It must be a different kind of love that allows us to fight them. To say that you can love your enemy while in a lawsuit against him is like saying you can love your enemy while dueling with him.

A person who oppresses us offends against justice; but

if we resist, we offend against meekness. And suffering can teach us obedience. The Scripture says of Christ, "But even though he was God's Son, he learned through his sufferings to be obedient" (Heb. 5:8). Now if God's only begotten Son, without sin, full of divine knowledge, received instruction from suffering, how much more must we need that learning!

To believe that we can know about obedience to God without suffering is to say we do not need the help the Son of God had. Sufferings ought to be considered among God's grace.

The same Letter to the Hebrews earlier says that Jesus was "crowned with honor and glory because of the death He suffered" and He was made "perfect through suffering" (Heb. 2:9–10). And Peter, speaking to servants, says, "If you endure suffering even when you have done right, God will bless you for it. It was to this that God called you, for Christ Himself suffered for you and left you an example, so that you would follow in His steps" (1 Pet. 2:20, 21).

These teachings may seem hard, but they seem so because we have wrong notions of human life. Too many of us imagine this life to be something valuable in itself, and religion something added to life to make it easier and more pleasant. We therefore embrace Christianity to the degree that it eases and comforts our lives.

Sufferings do not only cause us no real hurt, however; they actually promote our happiness and become the cause for real and solid joy. "Happy are you when people insult you and persecute you and tell all kinds of evil lies against you because you are My followers. Be happy and glad, for a great reward is kept for you in heaven" (Matt. 5:11–12).

Christ does not try to comfort us in suffering by telling us how patience makes it easier to bear this hard state. He looks at it from another view, not as a situation needing comfort, but as a matter fit for congratulations. What strangers are we to Christ's spirit who reckon as a hardship what He recommends to us as a reason for rejoicing?

If suffering and self-denial make us more like Christ, they have done more for us than wealth can do. Whoever defends himself at the expense of losing Christ's attitude has done himself a far worse injury than his enemy did.

# Chapter 8
*Self-Denial*


Self-denial is reasonable. Christian virtues are required because they are good and reasonable things to be done, not simply because God has the power to command what He pleases. If we are commanded to be humble, it is because humility is a suitable attitude for a dependent being.

If we are commanded to rejoice, it is at something truly joyful. If we are commanded to fear, it is to fear something truly dreadful. We are called to true attitudes as if being called to believe that two is half of four.

God does not lie. And God does not ask us to love things horrible or hate things lovely. God is perfectly reasonable. He therefore only wills that His reasonable creatures be more reasonable and perfect—more like Himself. He will place on us no duties or attitudes unless they have this tendency. All His commands are for our own sakes and are really instructions in how to be happier than we would be without them.

We declare people insane when they imagine themselves to be something different from what they really are. We consider people fools who do not know the real value of things. An unbelieving sinner is thus insane and foolish; he does not recognize what he is and he mistakes the value of things. Christianity is our education. It teaches us who we are and the true value of everything.

Some people, either through self-love or confusion, imagine themselves to be particularly in God's favor. They imagine their worldly success to be evidence of God's special blessing. But success in this life is hardly a mark of God's favor. "The Lord corrects everyone He loves, and punishes everyone He accepts as a son" (Heb. 12:6). The successful people who do not understand this verse are far from understanding the necessity for humility and self-denial. These people do not understand that humility is a more reasonable attitude than the belief that God always showers His children with worldly success.

All Christian duties and attitudes are ultimately reasonable. For instance, humility is simply a correct judgment of ourselves. To think worse of ourselves than we really are is no more of a virtue than pretending five to be less than four. To think better of ourselves than we really are is equally foolish.

Why is self-denial reasonable? Suppose that, for some reason, a lady has to walk on a rope high above a raging river. She is told while walking to deny herself the distraction of looking around at the beautiful waves. She is not to dress in fancy high heels or fish for trout during her walk. Would she feel these restrictions to be a hardship? Wouldn't denying herself be a reasonable thing?

"The gate to life is narrow, and the way that leads to it is hard," Jesus said (Matt. 7:14). If Christians are to walk on a narrow way, it behooves us to deny ourselves things that might lead us to fall. If we think self-indulgence is consistent with trying to keep on that narrow way, we might as reasonably think the lady on the rope could wear heels or fish for trout.

This is the foundation of Christian self-denial: In order to gain virtues, we try to avoid distractions. A person who wants to be healthy doesn't just take medicine; he avoids things that might make him sick.

One example of overindulgence is the sin of overeating, called gluttony. Gluttony is often difficult to define. However, a person who admits he has eaten so much Sunday dinner that he does not feel like doing anything except taking a nap—that person has spoken against himself.

Some people think gluttony means you have to eat yourself sick. But Scripture has a surer guide: "Whatever you do, whether you eat or drink, do it all for God's glory" (1 Cor. 10:31). A person who stuffs himself wants only to be idle, not to glorify God.

Christ spoke of how to fast at the same time He told how to pray and give alms. "When you go without food, wash your face and comb your hair, so that others cannot know that you are fasting—only your Father, who is unseen, will know. And your Father, who sees what you do in private, will reward you" (Matt. 6:17–18). The same instruction and the same reasons are given for fasting as for almsgiving and private prayer.

Some people object that fasting is not a duty for all time. If by fasting they mean complete abstinence from food for a given period, I would agree. But I understand fasting to be abstinence from harmful, improper, excessive food, and thus appropriate for today.

Paul said, "I harden my body with blows and bring it under complete control, to keep myself from being disqualified after having called others to the contest" (1 Cor. 9:27). He was not undergoing self-denial to receive more spiritual gifts, but for the sake of his salvation. This mighty apostle thought his other virtues insecure without self-control.

# Chapter 9
*Natural Corruption*

Two truths stand out in the Scriptures: the general corruption of human nature and the absolute necessity of divine grace. Our corruption is like an illness. Either we are applying medicine (grace) to it and weakening it, or else by ignoring it we let it grow stronger.

We can thus evaluate our spiritual health. If we are denying ourselves, we are becoming stronger. But if we are in a state of self-love, we are not.

Sometimes when we speak of self-denial, we are thinking only of the obvious, sensual sins. But the most difficult sins to watch against are those of the spirit, such as self-love and pride. If we deny ourselves in some areas but indulge ourselves in others, we will be a curious and futile mixture. We must lay the axe to the root of the tree, denying not only individual pleasures but our whole indulgent natures, giving ourselves up to the Sprit of God.

Suppose Christianity required us to forget the language that we had grown up with and to learn to speak only a difficult new language. Could we possibly forget our natural language any other way than refusing to ever let ourselves speak it? Could we forget it by only using it occasionally? Wouldn't we have to keep, not only from speaking in it, but from reading, writing, and even thinking in it?

This can teach us the necessity of universal self-denial. Though Christianity does not command us to part with an old language, it does command us to part with an old nature and live in a new spirit. To get rid of the old nature, we must not only stop acting by it, but even liking, disliking, thinking, and wishing by it.

An examination of human nature and Christian nature convinces us that self-denial of the old nature is the beginning of virtue. Christianity teaches us three main principles. First, God is our only good, and we cannot be happy except in Him. Second, our souls are immortal spirits, here on trial. Third, we must all appear before God's judgment seat to receive a sentence of eternal life or eternal death.

Every Christian is to live according to these principles, judging and thinking, choosing and avoiding, hoping and fearing, hating and loving according to them. We live as creatures sent here to prepare to live with God in everlasting happiness.

This makes all of Christianity a self-denial, a contradiction to our natural ideas. What could be more contradictory to our habitual notions than happiness in God alone? It is a happiness which our senses, those familiar guides, can neither see, hear, nor taste.

Look at the natural man. He acts as if the world contains infinite varieties of happiness. He has a thousand pleasures and a thousand irritations, which show he thinks happiness can be found everywhere. For who gets irritated unless he thinks he has been cheated of some happiness? So Christianity is an obvious self-denial; it leads us from the enjoyments our senses have labeled happiness to a good our senses cannot perceive.

Our senses can tell us when to sleep, how close to get to a fire, and how much we can carry; they are proper guides in these things. But if we consult them regarding guilt, happiness, and excellence, it is like trying to hear with eyes or see with ears. Concerning the value of things, adults have the same judgment as children. We laugh at children's wishes for small trifles, but we fill our own thoughts with large trifles. When an adult thinks how happy he would be if he could just win a lottery or sweepstakes, that is just like the child who wishes he had enough money to buy twenty sticks of candy.

A person who has filled his mind with alcohol cannot think reasonably. One might as well not attempt a serious conversation with him. And a person who has filled his mind with sports, or fashion, or gossip, cannot think reasonably from a Christian point of view. He fails to perceive the pleasures of spiritual conversation.

# Chapter 10
*The Holy Spirit*

The Holy Spirit makes us want to do good and enables us to do it.

Our natural lives are preserved by God, but we can't perceive His life-sustaining influence. The same is true of the Holy Spirit for our spiritual life. Jesus said, "The wind blows wherever it wishes; you hear the sound it makes, but you do not know where it comes from or where it is going. It is like that with everyone who is born of the Spirit" (John 3:8). We can feel the Holy Spirit's effects, as we can see the wind's effects; but we can't tell how he comes upon us.

According to Paul, "Those who are led by God's Spirit are God's sons" (Rom. 8:14). This shows that we must cooperate with the Holy Spirit. Rocks will not allow seeds to grow, and stony hearts will not bring forth the fruits of the Holy Spirit.

Everyone acknowledges that drunks and criminals cannot produce spiritual fruit. But neither can a mind busy with worldly cares. Why are little children incapable of Spirit-filled Christianity? It is not because they are drunks and criminals, but simply that their minds are always occupied with trifles. If as adults we have merely exchanged mental playthings, we can hardly expect sustained spiritual growth.

Philip goes to church and reads the Bible, but he doesn't get much out of it because his head is full of politics. He gets so irritated with his senators and representatives that he makes no effort to examine himself. His thoughts continually dwell on elections and legislation. Eugenia is the same way about business, and Sam is the same way about sports. It is not just gross sins, but any succession of worldly thoughts that can keep us from having time to listen to the Holy Spirit.

If you attempt to talk with a dying man about sports or business, he is no longer interested. He now sees other things as more important. People who are dying recognize what we often forget, that we are standing on the brink of another world.

The Holy Spirit is working in our hearts to give us a new understanding. To the extent that we nourish old passions, we resist the Holy Spirit. We make ourselves less likely to delight in His inspirations. We must be free of false hopes to rejoice in the Spirit's comforts.

A man may go hear comedians and laugh at their jokes, but if he is peevish and grouchy the rest of the time, no one would call him good-humored. And if we are very devout in church, but frivolous away from church, we can hardly be called Christians. If a greedy person prays generous prayers, he is still greedy. And if a person is reverent in a daily prayer but never thinks of God any other time, he is not a Christian.

People talk as they think. Sports fans, in normal conversation, say, "You've thrown me a curve there" and "I'll have to punt my way out of this situation." Television fans use the phrases of their favorite characters. And committed Christians will find their speech punctuated with references to Christ. They will talk with like-minded people about the same subjects, whether at church or in homes.

When a pastor preaches, people consider him to be simply doing his job. All preachers preach, but if he is as edifying in normal speech as in the pulpit, people will take more notice of the sermons. What he says through the week will add weight to what he says on Sunday. Conversely, a pastor who always trifles in conversation lessens his power of influencing his hearers.

Parents occasionally try to advise a son or daughter about the importance of Christianity. This will do the child good if he hears his parents speak highly of Christianity —and act it out—at other times. But if they only praise Christianity when they are advising him to follow it, he thinks they are only doing a parental duty, much like providing food and clothes.

A mother teaches her daughter Bible stories. The daughter likes the Bible stories, but notices that Mommy, in her own reading, is most interested in romances and homemaking magazines. The daughter is educated by what the mother does. Our conversation and ordinary life affect the people living around us. We will either let them harden in sin or we will alert them to Christianity.

# Chapter 11
## *Trashy Reading*

Reading on wise and virtuous subjects is, next to prayer, the best improvement of our hearts. It enlightens us, calms us, collects our thoughts, and prompts us to better efforts. We say that a man is known by the friends he keeps; but a man is known even better by his books.

It is reckoned dangerous not to guard our eyes; it is even more dangerous not to guard our reading. What we read enters more deeply than what we happen to see. Reading is to our souls what food is to our bodies; we can do ourselves much good or much harm by our choices.

You might think it dull to read Christian books. But when you come to find in God your only happiness, you will think Christian books the most exciting. To a Spirit-filled person, Christian books are a feast and joy for the mind.

But trashy novels and romances! If you have spare time, use it for taking a nap or playing mumblety-peg instead. They'll do you less harm than reading trash.

And after all, where did we come up with this concept of "spare time," anyway? Is there any time for which we aren't accountable to God? Is there any time during which God doesn't care what you are doing? *No Christian has ever had spare time.* You may have spare time from labor or necessity, you may stop working and refresh yourself, but no Christian ever had time off from living like a Christian.

You have time to recreate and refresh yourself, but that time is to be governed by Christian wisdom. Many people are doomed to such hardship that they can rarely choose what they want to do. But if you have "spare time," you have the power to choose the best thing, the best ways of life, opportunities for self-improvement.

A scriptural teaching that seems quite reasonable is, "Much is required from the person to whom much is given" (Luke 12:48). A life with leisure time affords great opportunities. Had you been born in a different time as a servant or slave, especially under a cruel master, you would have been doing God's work simply by dedicating your daily toil to God. Being free of that burden, you should look on yourself as God's servant, spending your time laboring after His desires. You have no more time of your own than a slave; but your Master gives you freedom to choose your means of service.

# Chapter 12
## Soap Operas and Pajama Comedies

Can a Christian watch soap operas and pajama comedies? Absolutely not, in my opinion. We would think it strange if a person who doesn't swear visits buildings simply to hear curses. It's equally ridiculous for modest men and women to sit and watch other men and women act immodestly. Non-Christians are understandably delighted with sexual wordplay, because they tell sexual jokes themselves. But for Christians who never tell sexual jokes to laugh at them on TV contradicts common sense.

When you see actors playing the parts of prostitutes and adulterers, do you believe them to be committed to Christ? Hardly. If an actor's part approves and encourages immodesty, that's as sinful as encouraging theft.

NOTE: During Law's early life, the most popular stage plays were witty sexual farces with double entendres, closet lovers, and other forms of titillation. The closest modern equivalent would be television's "pajama comedies." (*Three's Company* is a familiar recent example.) Since Law's ire is directed toward sexual titillation in drama, this edition of his book refers to pajama comedies and soap operas to make his point. The chapter's concluding couplet originally appeared in an eighteenth-century magazine (*The Spectator,* Number 79) and has been modernized for this edition.

115

What is modesty? Is it outside behavior or an inward attitude? If modesty is only outside behavior, then I can see how a person who acts modestly himself could delight in others' immodesty. But I can't comprehend how a person who wants every thought pure would seek out soap operas or even remain in the room while they're on.

Do not misunderstand me. When I say a pajama comedy is immodest, I do not mean every person who watches a pajama comedy is also immodest. (I think astrology makes no sense, but that doesn't mean every believer in astrology has no sense.) The way we have been raised may influence us to do something that does not fit our general principles. But, as I already said, I cannot understand how a person seeking to live a holy life could waste time watching soap operas or other sex-saturated programs.

I once heard a woman excuse herself about watching soap operas by saying she only watched them with her family. "I still go to church and read my Bible," she said. "Soap operas don't cut into my time too much. They never interfere with my daily devotions."

That hardly comes to the point. A good many wicked things could be done without cutting into her "quiet times." The question is how these shows affect her attitudes. Does her watching accord with God's will, and is it appropriate for one led by the Spirit of Christ? If so, she could watch the show with her family or without. If not, then it certainly doesn't make the situation better to have her family watch with her. We do not make a bad thing right by calling it "family time." This lady would hardly tell her pastor, "I occasionally get drunk, but only with my family."

If watching soap operas is a harmless and useful means of recreation, like walking, bike-riding, exercise, or good conversation, the lady need not excuse herself at all. If it's bad, then it hardly helps that she does it rarely. We would laugh at someone who said, "I occasionally commit adultery, but I still go to church and read my Bible. Adultery doesn't cut into my time too much. It never interferes with my daily devotions."

Suppose you had never seen a soap opera before. You are a Christian and want to evaluate it by scriptural principles. So first you ask what a soap opera is. You are told it is a performance in which actors try to move viewers emotionally with dialogues and action. The scripts (you are told) are written by intelligent, imaginative writers. These scripts primarily describe imaginary intrigues and love scenes. The dialogues center on lust and passion. They are performed by actors trained to present lustful passion in an appealing way.

You would not, in your Bible, find a commandment specifically against this activity. But you would certainly judge it to be out of keeping with the nature of Christianity.

True indeed were the gentleman's words:

*Her right eye views the Word, her left the soaps;*
*She gives both God and Satan equal hopes.*

# Chapter 13
*Real Christianity*

So many people tend to confuse religious devotion and religious emotion. Consider a woman at a Christian concert. She is (to her mind) joyful in God's praise and fervent in worship. But her fervor may be due more to the intensity of the music than to true worship. An emotional high does not necessarily constitute genuine devotion to God.

Nor is the search for correctness in Christian belief necessarily a sign of the person's zeal for God. John is very concerned for correct doctrine. He is always eager to read books and pamphlets against cults and other denominations. There is only one type of religious book he doesn't care for, and that is anything on personal devotion. He has no keen interest in books on humility, love, heavenly-mindedness, self-denial, or kindness.

Many people are like John in this respect. They always want more instruction *on certain points*. They will read certain books, but they can't bear to be instructed about any matter in which they are possibly mistaken, to their spiritual detriment. They are grateful if you tell them the dates that the Gospels were written. They are thankful for you explaining the words *rabboni* or *Anathema Maranatha*.

They are glad for such "useful" instruction. But if you touch upon matters that really concern them, these religious people, so fond of religious truth, cannot bear to be instructed.

Alas, so many intelligent people become preoccupied with dates and linguistic problems concerning the Bible that they have no time to seriously consider the Bible's main theme, God's love for us and our loving response to Him. They seem so concerned for truth, yet neglect the real purpose of truth, which is to bring us closer to the God of truth.

Why do we consult lawyers? Is it to hear lectures on legal codes? To hear about legal disputes? No, indeed, we consult them because we want assistance on our own case. To further that end, we give them all the information we can.

Why do we go to doctors? To learn about medical history? To hear of other people's diseases? No, we want a cure for our own. And we are glad for them to examine every part of our lives, even how we eat and sleep.

Why do we act this way toward doctors and lawyers? Because we're serious about the matter. And when we are serious about Christianity, we are equally glad to have our lives examined. Serious Christians are more concerned with rooting out sin and growing in grace than in maintaining an emotional high or resolving all the scholarly questions about Christian doctrine. So we read the books and consult the people who are most effective in finding corruption and leading to health. If we don't act this way, if we try to cover up what we think and say and do, we are not serious about moving toward Christian perfection.

# Chapter 14
*Prayer*

Our Savior is now at the right hand of God, interceding for us. Knowing this should encourage our prayers. When we pray, we are doing on earth what Christ is perpetually doing for us in heaven. Since our prayers are only acceptable to God through the merits of Jesus Christ, we pray to God in the most prevailing way when we remember Christ's name and His merits.

Devotion may be considered either as voiced prayers, public and private, or as an attitude of the heart. External devotion only has value when it proceeds from internal devotion. When Christians are asked to pray without ceasing, this refers to the inward state; we cannot be every moment voicing prayers. In the same way, we confess our faith only at certain times, but the faith stays with us always.

The reason for prayer is found in God's nature and our nature. God is the sole fountain of happiness; humans are weak and full of needs. Prayer, then, is an application or ascent of the heart to God as the cause of all happiness. The person who prays most fervently is the one who most realizes both his weakness and God's power to relieve sorrow. To be filled with a prayerful spirit, we must know ourselves. When we lose track of our own littleness or of God's greatness, or when we think pleasure can be found anywhere besides God, we lose our state of devotion. We can only desire what we feel we need. If we feel less needy, then we become less fervent for God's relief.

Sometimes we tell people to be more fervent in prayer. That does as much good as telling people to be happy or sad. People wear their attitudes based on their evaluations of circumstances. If they perceive things to be going well, they will be happy; if they perceive things to be going poorly, they will be sad; if they perceive their lives to be empty, they will be fervent in prayer. A person generally does not grieve when life goes well; he doesn't rejoice when life goes poorly; and he doesn't long for God when he is satisfied with life.

Suppose you were to call a man away from a sumptuous feast. You tell him to go into the next room and be hungry for a half hour; then he can go back to feasting. You tell him he must really feel this hunger deeply.

He might obey you by going into the hunger room. He might even sit there licking his lips for a half hour. But the man is not really hungry. Why not? Because he has just come from a feast, and he is returning to a feast, and that dulls one's appetite.

This is the position of a great many Christians. They are always at a feast—a feast of pleasure and satisfaction. Then they go to Scripture and are told to hunger after God as their only real satisfaction. But their appetite is already dulled. If any person is perplexed to find himself not often hungering for God, he should explore the likely reason: He is already full.

Many people would like to pray fervently, so they read books on prayer and try to be more emotional. But they haven't taken the only possible way to become more fervent: altering their lives, which must involve our refusal to treasure worldly pleasures. We cannot live one way and pray another. It is like a woman expecting to become athletic by reading sports books and wishing she were so.

When Julia prays, she confesses herself to be a sinner. She repeats the words of Scripture, "I know that good does not live in me—that is, in my human nature" (Rom. 7:18). Yet Julia cannot bear to be informed of any imperfection. Could there be a stronger proof that Julia's prayers are insincere? If a woman were to admit to being lame, she would not be angry with those who offered her assistance.

Religious devotion means what it sounds like—being devoted to God. A devoted soul constantly rises toward God with habits of love, trust, hope, and joy. Actually, a person is not so much exhorted as carried into devotion. Consider these enlivening texts:

"But we know that when Christ appears, we shall be like him, for we shall see him as he really is" (1 John 3:2).

"Just as we wear the likeness of the man made of earth, so we will wear the likeness of the Man from heaven" (1 Cor. 15:49).

"Let us give thanks to the God and Father of our Lord Jesus Christ! Because of His great mercy He gave us new life by raising Jesus Christ from death" (1 Pet. 1:3).

"He will change our weak mortal bodies and make them like His own glorious body, using that power by which He is able to bring all things under His rule" (Phil. 3:21).

These truths shine a light on the soul that will kindle it into flames of love for God. The way to live devotion is to contemplate these thoughts continually. They will enable our little anxieties and selfish desires to be swallowed up in one great desire of future glory.

This type of devotion is in Scripture called living by faith and not by sight (2 Cor. 5:7). The invisible things of the future life determine our desires. This devotion makes us eager to pray; and our prayers in turn enliven our devotion.

People who like music want to go to concerts, and the concerts give them a greater appreciation for the music. People who desire to be with God pray, and prayer increases their delight in God. We can judge the sincerity of our prayers by our daily attitudes; we can judge our daily attitude by our fervency in prayer.

Some people think we need only pray for short periods of time. But continuance in prayer is stressed nearly as often in Scripture as prayer itself. Jesus gave the parable of the unjust judge to "teach them [the disciples] that they should always pray and never become discouraged" (Luke 18:1). Paul does not just command us to pray, but to "pray at all times" (1 Thess. 5:17). And in Colossians 4:2, the same apostle says, "Be persistent in prayer."

No one can specify how long a person ought to pray. But a person whose daily prayer lasts fifteen minutes or less has a definite disadvantage. The cares and distractions of life make us all more or less unprepared for devotion. If our time of prayer is short, we end our prayers before our devotion has really begun. It often takes several minutes to collect our minds and turn our hearts to the business at hand. A longer time for prayer gives the heart leisure to fall away from worldly concerns and exercises the mind.

All of us are inconstant in our prayers. We heartily attend some spiritual thoughts; our minds wander away from others. It is therefore common sense to extend our prayer times, to give our wandering minds an opportunity to rejoin us. A person who always prays for a short time, in a hurry, may pray his whole life without experiencing real devotion. If a person were to think, before beginning to pray, what prayer is, what he is praying for, and to whom he is praying, he would gain a more devout mind. I do not intend this, or anything else, as a specific rule for an effective prayer. This is only to show that there are ways to assist our devotion.

There are two seasons of our hearts when we can particularly learn about ourselves and how to foster our devotional lives: the times when we are most involved in prayer and the times when we least want to pray. Think about what happened the last time you had a really effective period of prayer. What circumstances were you in? What had you been doing? What were your thoughts? If you find out what made that prayer time so effective, you may be able to raise your devotion at other times. If you write down for occasional review things that stimulate your prayer time, you will find your efforts well rewarded.

And, from the other side, think about the last time your prayers were hindered. What thoughts were in your head? What had you done or intended to do? What emotions were you feeling? If you can figure out what hindered your prayers, you can make efforts to avoid it. If certain thoughts or subjects distract your mind from prayer, you have information on how to alter your life. Things that lower our minds will be daily guarded against by those who want to be daily alive to God.

Frequent and prolonged prayer aids in spiritual improvement. In praying we renew our convictions, enlighten our minds, and fortify our hearts. The benefit of prayer is not only that God hears it, but that it alters us. Some people argue for short prayers by observing that God does not need to hear our lives discussed at length. True enough, God doesn't; but *we* do. It does not take much prayer to move God, but it takes a great deal to move us.

If God does not give us something at the first asking, if He waits until later, it is not because our prayers have made any change in God. But prayer makes a change in ourselves, for it renders us ready for God's grace.

Prayer is most effective when we specify our needs and imperfections. Of course, God does not need to be informed of them, but it informs us. We see ourselves more truly. When we detail all our circumstances and thoughts, we are making a mirror for our lives; God's light shines on the mirror and lets us see ourselves.

Don't contentedly confess yourself a sinner in general; this only shows you to be a human being, for we are all sinners. Lay open your sins specifically. Seeing them in God's light will influence you to amend your life. And don't just pray for "grace to be better," but ask the Holy Spirit to aid you in those specific areas you most lack.

Being specific puts truth in our prayers. A person might think he really wants humility if he asks for it in general terms. But if he begins asking for grace to be humble in a variety of specific situations, he may discover himself not to be so eager for it after all. If he were in prayer to look to instances of people being poor in spirit, he may find he doesn't have a real desire to be like that. The only way to know if our hearts are true when we pray for virtues is to ask for them regarding specific situations.

If a greedy man were to beg God daily to frustrate his attempts to become wealthier, one of two things would happen: The greed would win and he would cease praying, or the prayers would win and he would cease being greedy. He could hardly continue in greed if every day he listed his moneymaking schemes, one by one, and asked God to topple them.

Anyone may grow spiritually from prayer if he earnestly desires to. Most people do not appear to know themselves; but we may know ourselves by presenting our lives to God in prayer.

Let me add one word more: The person who learns to really pray learns the greatest secret of a holy and happy life. God is suited to our natures. He is equal to our needs, a constant source of comfort and refreshment. He will fill us with peace and joyful expectations here and eternal happiness hereafter. The man whose heart is full of God lives at the top of human happiness. He is furthest removed from those disturbances that vex the minds of worldly men.

# Chapter 15
*Imitating Jesus Christ*

"Just as we wear the likeness of the man made of earth, so we will wear the likeness of the Man from heaven" (1 Cor. 15:49). Since Christianity intends us to be like Jesus in the afterlife, it is no wonder we are expected to be like Jesus in this life.

We are called to imitate Christ. This does not mean performing all of His exact actions, but having His attitudes. Just as no doctrines are Christian unless they fit Christ's teaching, no life is Christian unless it fits Christ's pattern.

Jesus said, "I am the way, the truth, and the life; no one comes to the Father except by Me" (John 14:6). Many Christians think they have fulfilled these words simply by believing in Jesus Christ. But as we must believe in His truth and receive from Him life, we must follow His way.

Jesus Christ came into the world to save the world. Salvation should also be our greatest concern, both for ourselves and others. Of course, we cannot contribute toward salvation what Jesus did. The work of salvation is carried on in a variety of ways. For an unlearned person to desire instruction may promote salvation as truly as for a teacher to instruct. That teachable attitude may draw others into learning as effectively as the teacher's ability. Often a teacher's success is due more to the people being taught than to his own strength. Any of us, no matter what our level of learning, can exemplify holiness and make our lives a lesson.

Christ is the Savior of the world. To be like Him, we must attempt to save others (although, as I said, we cannot save in the sense that He did). Paul said, "How can you be sure, Christian wife, that you will not save your husband? Or how can you be sure, Christian husband, that you will not save your wife?" (1 Cor. 7:16). Paul clearly thinks it a possibility that we can have a share in our spouse's salvation. If this is true about a spouse, why not another relative, a friend, a neighbor?

Troy is a devout Christian who always tries to be around other devout Christians. He avoids being with unbelievers whenever possible. Troy has failed to realize that this is like a doctor avoiding sick people. We cannot be dutiful Christians if our concern for our own purity makes us neglect our duty to witness to unbelievers. All of us are hired to work in Christ's vineyard.

Claude has his head full of future Christianity. He often thinks what he would do if he were extremely rich. He would not spend it all on himself like other millionaires, but would give huge portions to charitable causes.

Claude presently has a middle-class income. He spends it the way other middle-class people do. He doesn't limit his comfort, but continually talks about how he would limit his spending if he were rich. Come to your senses, Claude! Do not talk about what you'd do if you were an angel instead of a man or a millionaire instead of middle-class. Do now what you would want to do if you were wealthy; deny yourself and be charitable.

Fred is a Christian businessman whose desire to do great things for God makes him overlook the little good things that are in his power. Fred often thinks how perfect life would be if he were a pastor; then he'd spend all his time caring for God and other people.

Don't believe it, Fred! Why do think you would spread the spirit of Christianity throughout a church when you aren't doing it in your own family? What about the people who work for you? If they do their jobs well, you never trouble your head about their Christianity. You open your restaurant before noon on Sundays, never asking your employees if this causes them to miss church. You think that as a clergyman you would lay down your life for the flock, yet you won't lay aside part of the Sunday dinner business for your employees. You're not called to be a martyr, Fred; you're only called to give up some profit to let your employees worship if they wish to do so.

Jeannie, you do not know whether you will have a family. But you have yourself right now. You think you will read Bible stories to your children; how often do *you* read the Bible now? You think you will pray with your little ones every day; how much do you pray now? You think your family's conversation will be filled with God; how much are your thoughts centered on God now? Changing your state from singleness to wife and mother will not alter your spiritual way of life.

People always please themselves with an imaginary perfection to be arrived at when their circumstances are better.

"I have come down from heaven," Jesus said, "to do not My own will but the will of Him who sent Me" (John 6:38). Was Jesus a loser by neglecting human happiness and devoting Himself to God's will? Can we be losers by devoting ourselves to God alone?

One further observation about imitating Christ. Nothing is more likely to fill us with Christlike attitudes than reading the Gospels, which contain His life and conversations. We usually think we have read a book well enough when we are not just reading to know what they contain, but to fill our hearts with their spirit. By constantly spending time with our Lord in His Word, we shall find our hearts hungering and thirsting after righteousness.

## Chapter 16
*Perfection*

WE exhort people to a good many things: studying poetry, becoming rich or famous, learning to use computers. If someone were to ask me why he should learn to use a computer, I would tell how it could benefit his life. But if he were to ask me what good computer knowledge would do after his life ended, I wouldn't have an answer. Only Christianity can stand the trial of that second question.

Pyrrhus, the king of ancient Epirus, told his counselor, Cineas, that he intended to conquer all the nations around him. "Why?" asked Cineas. "What will we do then?"

"We will live without fear and enjoy ourselves and our friends," replied Pyrrhus.

"Then, sir," asked Cineas, "why don't we live without fear now?"

Suppose we were to ask a Christian what he will do when he gets the wealth or education or position he wants. He would probably say he intends to be close to God. Then why not be close to God now?

Only a true dedication of ourselves to Christianity can make it fully pleasant for us. When we are divided between God and the world, we don't have the pleasures of either.

We have enough Christianity to check our worldly enjoyments and interrupt our entertainments, but not enough to let us taste their satisfactions. We don't dare neglect Christianity; but we are as hesitant to pursue it fully as we are fearful to pursue the world fully. We are as unhappy as a slave who serves his master grudgingly but doesn't dare run away. The only reason many people can tolerate Christianity is because it doesn't take up much time.

Earl goes to church. He can't understand people who don't believe in God; he also can't understand people who live for God daily. Earl accepts religion because it seems like an easy way to please God. It doesn't take up much time and is such a decent thing to be involved with. But when Earl thinks of happiness or delight, he certainly doesn't think of religion. He continues for years in a practice that does him no real harm—nor good.

Let me exhort you, if you're going to profess Christianity, to devote yourself wholly to God. You may then have the peace of a unified heart.

Christian perfection involves overcoming difficulties. You could not love your neighbors if you had no neighbors to love. And you could not attempt to overcome the world if it had no temptation. If all the people you knew were devout, humble, and heavenly-minded, it would involve no overcoming to be like them. But to be humble among the proud and devout among the worldly takes effort. It is ridiculous to say we would be devoted to God if our position weren't so difficult; *every* position in this world is difficult.

We look at other believers in God, good churchgoing people, who live a "normal" life. We think God can't reject so many religious people, so we'll be safe if we're like them. We don't know in the case of any other churchgoer whether he is bound for heaven or hell. But when Christ has said, "But the gate to life is narrow, and the way that leads to it is hard, and there are few people who find it" (Matt. 7:14), it's foolish to complacently glide along with the majority. Alas, the majority of religious people are too much occupied with seeking earthly happiness.

Heavenly happiness is far more secure than earthly happiness. Bad luck or misfortune cannot keep us from heavenly happiness, nor malice by our enemies, nor betrayal by our friends. If our hearts remain true, neither life nor death, nor supernatural beings nor men, can separate us from the happiness of God.

# HOLY LIVING
## AND
# HOLY DYING

JEREMY TAYLOR

# JEREMY TAYLOR (1613–1667)

One of the greatest preachers of all time, Jeremy Taylor was born in Cambridge, England, in 1613. He was educated at Cambridge University and was for a time imprisoned during the Civil War for his loyalty to the king. Upon his release he served for many years as chaplain at Golden Grove, where he wrote his major works, including *The Liberty of Prophesying* (1651). He also wrote the devotional *Exercises of Holy Dying* (1651) and the devotional manual *The Golden Grove* (1655). Taylor later pastored churches in London and in Ireland, where he died in 1667.

Taylor's sermons are still worth reading for their eloquence and breadth of learning. His theological works are also written in an engaging, elegant style, a style that reflects his love of beauty and God's order. But he is best remembered for his two devotional masterpieces, *Holy Living* and *Holy Dying*. In these two books he was able to accomplish two difficult tasks: make the life of Christian holiness seem attractive and make the Christian see that death is an inevitable good for those who live and die for God.

# Chapter 1
*Care of Our Time*

God has given to man only a short time upon the earth, and yet upon this short time eternity depends. Thus for every hour of our lives (after we reach the age of knowing good from evil) we must give account to the great Judge. This is what our blessed Savior meant when He said we must give account for every careless word (Matt. 12:36). He didn't mean that any word not specifically designed for edification will be reckoned a sin; He meant that the time we spend in idle talk and useless conversation—the time that could have been used for spiritual and useful purpose—that time is to be accounted for.

We need not fear that this carefulness of time must be a continual vexation to us, for the entire life of everyone can be a perpetual serving of God. The busiest job, when it is necessary or charitable, can be done in God's service. God provides for our needs through the labor of the farmer, the skill of the craftsman, and the commerce of the merchant. These people, through their daily work, can be ministers of God, stewards of creation, and servants of God's world-family. They are employed by Him in providing food, clothing, shelter, and medicine. In the same way, legislators, pastors, and judges are doing the work of God when they do their work rightly, for they are serving needs which God has provided for through their ministry.

Thus no one can truly complain that his job takes him away from religion. Any honest job is in itself a service for God if it is pursued with moderation and leaves sufficient time for meditation and prayer. Whoever has the fewest job obligations is called on to spend more time fitting his soul. Whoever has the most work duties may still make them a service for God, as long as his work is blessed by prayer and hallowed with holy intentions.

Idleness is the greatest waste in the world. It throws away something irreplaceable, for we have no possible way of recovering our time. To improve our use of time we may practice the following principles.

*Guidelines for Using Our Time Wisely*

1. In the morning, when you awaken, accustom yourself to think first upon God; and at night, let Him close your eyes. Let your rest be healthful and necessary, not just idle time.
2. Let all your intervals or open moments of time be employed in prayer, reading, meditation, exercise, and acts of friendship.
3. Sundays and holidays are in no sense mere days of idleness. It is better to work on Sundays than to do nothing. Instead of idly wasting time, let those days be spent doing charitable and religious work.
4. Avoid the company of all who talk too much without a purpose. No one can be careful in his use of time who is careless in his choice of company, for when a conversationalist continually speaks emptiness or trivia, all who listen or answer waste their time.

5. Never engage in any trifling activity merely to pass the time away, for every day well spent can become a "day of salvation" (2 Cor. 6:2 NIV), and any time rightly used is an "opportune moment" (Ps. 69:13). The time you trifle away was given to you to repent, to pray, to lay up heavenly treasure.

6. While working, go often to God in brief prayers. These times of prayer can make up the lack of devotional time which others may have and which you wish you had. Be sure of this: God is as present at your breathed prayers on the job as at the longer prayers of those who are less employed.

7. Let your employment be fitting for a reasonable person. A person may be idle though busy. There are entire occupations devoted to vanity and foolishness that deserve to be banned. And there are some people who are genuinely busy, but it is in the way the Emperor Domitian once claimed to be busy: catching flies.

8. Let those who are independently wealthy or retired be extra careful in their use of time. Let them choose good company and learn useful things. Let them visit the poor and relieve their needs, pray often, and read good books.

9. Everyone should avoid excessive attention to appearance. Many people primp and comb away all their opportunities for morning devotions.

10. People should avoid idle curiosity and inquiring into things that do not concern them. Of course, we should be aware of the needs of our fellow believers, but one need not be a gossip to learn his brothers' needs.

11. As much as possible, cut off all useless occupations of your life: unnecessary meetings, daydreaming, reading about celebrities, or however time is spent to no real purpose.

12. Do not spend time lavishly in recreation, but choose leisure activities that are healthful, brief, and refreshing. Avoid games that require too much time or involvement, or which are likely to dominate your thoughts. Do not dwell upon them or make them your major enterprises. And don't think that spectator sports are real exercise. A person who passively spends his time watching sports and calls it exercise makes about as much sense as a person who wears a belt without wearing any pants. It is permissible to relax our bow but not to unstring it.

13. Set aside some parts of every day specifically for prayer and devotion. Events may force you to shorten your devotional time occasionally, but do not omit it under anything less than absolute necessity.

14. Do God's work attentively. Do not let your hands be folded in prayer while your thoughts are on the world. Do not pray negligently. Put forth all your strength.

15. Fill hours of insomnia with prayer, since you have no requirements on your time then.

16. The busy person should set aside a holy time every year in which, ignoring his occupation, he may give himself wholly to fasting and prayer, to confession and attention to God.

17. Before we sleep we might well examine our actions during the day, especially anything unusual. For our failures we will have sorrow, and for our victories we will have thanksgiving.

18. All these points should be used wisely, not vex-ingly. These guidelines have advantages, but they are not divine commandments, at least not their specifics. Every person may select whatever process enables him to do his Christian duty. A man will be happy when he can use every hour in a useful or holy way, but our duty does not consist in just scrupulously examining how we use our minutes (provided no minute is engaged in sin).

19. The habit of using time wisely will influence our whole lives, and will especially benefit us in two ways. It doesn't just teach us to avoid evil but encourages us to do good. And it causes us to be ready and eager for the Lord's return at any time.

# Chapter 2
*Pure Intentions*

We should intend God's glory in every action we do. Paul expressed it this way: "Whether you eat or drink or whatever you do, do it all for the glory of God" (1 Cor. 10:31 NIV). When we observe that rule, every natural act becomes worshipful. Blessed is the goodness and grace of God! Out of infinite desire to save mankind, He makes even our most human acts capable of virtue, so that all our lifetime we may do Him service.

Intending God's glory is so excellent that it sanctifies our most common actions and so necessary that without it our very best acts of devotion are imperfect. A man who prays because others expect him to, or who gives money for praise, is a Pharisee and hypocrite. But a holy intention gains acceptance with God.

Choosing a holy end distinguishes good from evil. Zachariah and Mary both questioned the angel Gabriel, but Zachariah was struck speechless, while Mary was held blameless. She questioned to inquire how the event would take place, but he questioned the event itself (Luke 1:11–20, 26–38).

If a man visits his sick friend out of affection, we approve, and so does God. But if he does it to be named in the will, he is a vulture, only watching for the carcass. The same action can be honest or dishonest; intention makes the separation.

Holy intention is to a man's actions what the soul is to the body, or the sun to the world; without these, the body is dead, the world is darkness, and the action is unprofitable.

*Guidelines for Our Intentions*

1. In every action reflect upon the end. In undertaking anything honestly, consider *why* you want to do it. Ask if your motivation is truly honorable.
2. Begin every action in the name of the Father, Son, and Holy Spirit. This causes us to be careful we are doing the action with God's permission.
3. Let every important action be begun with prayer. Make the action an offering to God.
4. Be careful that what begins well, intended for God's glory, does not decline and end in your own praise. It is good in preaching to give an illustration of the evil of unchastity. But if your listeners become caught up with the story itself, and you begin to tell the story to receive laughter or praise rather than to illustrate evil, be careful. Like Nebuchadnezzar's image (Dan. 2:31–33), this act may have a head of gold, but descend in silver and brass, and end in iron and clay.
5. If you are tempted by an aspect of your religious duty, do not omit the duty, but instead try to purify your intention. Saint Bernard taught us this rule. Satan observed how much Bernard's excellent preaching benefited the hearers, so he

tempted Bernard to pride, hoping Bernard would stop preaching to avoid that sin. But Bernard answered Satan, "I did not begin this for you, so neither will I end it for you."

Many times a person's heart may deceive him; therefore I have a list of signs to show whether our intentions are pure and holy.

*Signs of Pure Intentions*

1. Our hearts are probably right with God when we value things properly. For instance, things necessary for our soul's health will be valued more highly than things for our body's health. When a person does recreation cheerfully and eagerly but does prayer and Bible study with reluctance, his heart clings too much to the world.
2. A person who does as well in private as in public is likely to have pure intentions. Whoever does good works for praise sells a valuable jewel for a trifle.
3. It is a good sign when we are not anxious about the outcome of our actions, but leave it to God's disposal in prayer. We are likely to be pure in purpose if we are indifferent regarding success. Saint James, according to an old tradition, converted only eight people when he preached in Spain, and our blessed Savior converted fewer people than His own disciples did. If your labors prove unsuccessful and your main concern is being a success, you are not working with pure intentions.
4. Whoever feels no attachment to the world is

most secure in his intentions because he is furthest removed from temptation. To the degree that we do not long for sensual pleasure and worldly reputation, to that degree we may conclude our hearts are spiritually right.

5. When we are not anxious about the means of accomplishing our ends but use thankfully the means God has given us, we are intent on God's glory rather than our own satisfaction. A person who does not care whether he serves God in wealth or poverty seeks God above himself.

6. When a temporary end consistent with our spiritual end happens to be defeated, but we can rejoice in that to secure God's glory, our hearts are right.

No good intention can sanctify an evil action. Those who killed the apostles had good purposes but unholy actions. We must have both right choices *and* loving intentions. A man who does evil for a good cause, or good for an evil cause, is like a thirsty man who roasts himself in a fire to quench his thirst with his own sweat. Consider not how full the hands are that you bring to God, but how pure.

## Chapter 3
*Practicing the Presence of God*

Remembering that God stands everywhere as both a witness and a judge should restrain our temptation much. Most outward sin is taken away if a person has a witness of his behavior. A man belittles God when, before doing something wrong, he first checks to make sure his children aren't around—as if the eye of a little child were more powerful than the all-seeing eye of the Lord!

God is to be feared in public and He is to be feared in private. The saints in heaven, who always behold the face of God, cannot sin. A remembrance of His presence would most quickly halt sin among us.

*Guidelines for Practicing God's Presence*

1. When you begin to pray, place yourself in God's presence and let your desires actually fix on Him. Then the rest of your prayer will more likely be wise.
2. Let everything you see represent God's presence, excellency, and power. In the face of the sun you may see God's beauty; in the fire you may feel His warmth; in the water you may feel His gentle refreshment.

3. Have frequent dialogues between God and your soul, as David did: "Seven times a day I praise you" (Ps. 119:164 NIV). Every act of thanksgiving, rejoicing, or mourning to God builds Him a chapel in our hearts. It reconciles Martha's employment with Mary's devotion (Luke 10:38–42). Even in the middle of your occupation you may worship at your heart-chapel.

4. As God is in us, we are in Him. We are His craftsmanship; let us not deface it. We are in His presence; let us not pollute it with unholy actions.

5. God created the animals. Do not be cruel to them or abuse them, but remember that the creatures are lesser receptacles of God's touch.

6. A person who walks with God, like Enoch, converses with Him in frequent prayer, runs to Him in every need, asks his advice whenever doubtful, weeps before Him for sin, and asks support for weakness. That person fears God as a Judge; reverences Him as a Lord; obeys Him as a Father; and loves Him as a Patron.

## The Benefits of Practicing God's Presence

1. Practicing God's presence produces a confidence in God, fearlessness toward enemies, patience in trouble, and hope of aid, since God is so near in all our circumstances. Though His rod of discipline may strike us, His staff supports us. He turns misery into mercy and trouble into advantage by showing us His presence in a new way.

2. Practicing God's presence produces joy in God, as we are more apt to delight in persons we know best. Every mutual conversation and togetherness becomes an endearment. If we walk

with God in all His ways as He walks with us in all ours, we will find perpetual reasons to "be joyful in the Lord always" (Phil. 4:4). This reminds me of a saying of Saint Anthony: "There is one way of overcoming our spiritual enemies —spiritual mirth and a perpetual bearing of God in our minds."

3. Practicing God's presence produces desire for God's strength, the same desire that a weak man has for a defender, a sick man for a doctor, and a child for a father.

4. Practicing God's presence produces spiritual humility, awareness of our great needs and His unfathomable mercies.

What a child would do under the eye of his father, a pupil before his teacher, and an employee before his boss, let us do, for we are always in the sight and presence of all-seeing and almighty God, our Father and Guardian, our Husband and Lord.

# Chapter 4
## *Christian Self-Control*

Christianity, according to Paul's arithmetic, has three parts to it: self-control, justice, religion. "For the grace of God that brings salvation has appeared to all men. It teaches us to say 'No' to ungodliness and worldly passions, and to live self-controlled, upright and godly lives in this present age" (Titus 2:11–12 NIV). The first part (being self-controlled) concerns us privately, the fair treatment of our bodies and spirits. The second (living uprightly) concerns our relations with our neighbors, and the third (being godly) concerns our relationship with God. This chapter and the four that follow focus on self-control.

Christian self-control involves matters of food and drink, pleasure, and thoughts. It contains the duties of (1) temperance, (2) chastity, (3) humility, (4) modesty, and (5) contentment. Self-control is any denial of unreasonable appetites.

*Suppressing Excessive Desire for Pleasure*

1. Accustom yourself to cutting off unnecessary desires in your life. As long as the things of this world are unsatisfying (that is, forever), your

desires will always be larger than your possessions. Even if you keep satisfying your desires,
they will still expand. But you can choose to
limit them. It is more important to control our
desires than to satisfy them.

2. Divert your desires by giving full attention to
something else. A person's mind cannot, at the
same time, wholly attend to two different
objects. Therefore if you give yourself to a book,
or a manual task, or any piece of mental involvement, you have no room left for sensual desire.

3. Look not on pleasures as they come smilingly
toward you to be enjoyed, but behold their
wearied appearance as they leave. I have known
some people who advise curing their children
of continual desire by letting them have everything they want. The children are sure to find
everything less enjoyable than anticipated.
Solomon tried all things, taking his fill of all
pleasures, and grew weary of them all. But we
may determine by reason what he had to learn
by experience.

4. Frequently contemplate the joys of heaven, for
such thoughts are the sails of the soul. When
your soul dwells above and looks from there
upon the pleasures of the world, they seem like
little things in the distance. People chasing after
pleasures seem as foolish as fish, thousands of
them, swimming after a wiggling worm on a
sharp hook. Or, at best, they are like noisy children chasing soap bubbles, bubbles that pop
even before the end of the children's noise.

The best method of self-control is to discover spiritual
pleasure. Spiritual pleasure is found in a good conscience,

a contented spirit, comforting hope, sweet devotion, and joyous thanksgiving. The more we delight in these, the more we will disregard earthly pleasures.

# Chapter 5
## *Temperance in Eating and Drinking*

If self-control is the bridle of desire, temperance is its bit, a restraint put into a man's mouth. Temperance is the moderate use of food and drink that agrees with our health, not hindering our souls but supporting and refreshing them.

Temperance permits eating and drinking, but only as they minister to the body. We should not eat and drink purely for pleasure, but for need and for refreshment, which is an element of need. Certainly eating and drinking may be done with pleasure; in a healthy body, they are always done with pleasure. There is in nature no greater pleasure than satisfying the legitimate desires created by God. It is permissible to receive delight and to plan to receive delight, as long as the chief reason is to serve some end for which refreshment is designed.

But when delight is the only end, and repeatedly the only end, then eating and drinking do not serve God; they are not being used in the way God intended. Choosing a special food over a more ordinary one is to be done in the same way other natural actions are to be done: wisely and moderately. Then God, who gives us such a variety of foods and the power to choose what we wish, receives glory both from our temperate use of those foods and our thanksgiving.

## Temperance in Eating

1. Do not eat before mealtime unless it is necessary or there is one valid reason to do so. It is inexcusable to stick your fork into the food before it's even ready, just because you are greedy for pleasure or impatient about delay.

2. Do not be a picky eater. Try not to be troublesome to others in having to have special meats or sauces. It was considered a sin for the people of Israel that they were not satisfied with manna but longed for meat; "The LORD became exceedingly angry" (Num. 11:10 NIV).

   And as far as preparation goes, Eli's sons were notorious for being picky; they wouldn't accept boiled meat but had to have it roasted (1 Sam. 2:12–15). Not that it was a sin to want to eat roast beef—but when it was supposed to be boiled as part of the tradition, they refused it. That indicated excessively picky taste. It is legitimate to be concerned about ingredients to protect a weak stomach, but not to please fastidious taste buds. Our health ought always to be provided for—but not our finicky cravings.

   "Eat whatever is put before you" (1 Cor. 10:27 NIV). If it has been provided for you, you may eat it, no matter how fancy. But if it's plain and common, as long as it's healthy, don't refuse it from pickiness.

3. Don't eat too much. A person should never overload his stomach. "Put a knife to your throat if you are given to gluttony" (Prov. 23:2 NIV).

*Signs of Temperance*

We can best know we have developed the virtue of temperance by the following signs, which are also arguments for its practice:

1. A temperate person is polite; greediness is rude. This is implied in the advice of Sirach: "Are you seated at a great table? Do not be the first to go after the food" (Ecclus. 31:12 [Apocrypha]).
2. Temperance remains calm; greediness becomes excited at the sight of delicacies.
3. A temperate person does not think or talk much of food and drink. He is healthy and has a long life (barring accidents), whereas illness is the continual companion of a glutton.

Besides maintaining temperance in yourself, never urge another person to eat or drink beyond his own limits. He who does so is a glutton from his brother's eating; they share the guilt.

# Chapter 6
*Chastity*

An introductory warning to be read before going on further: "To the pure, all things are pure" (Titus 1:15 NIV).

Reader, wait, and do not read the advice in the following section unless you have a chaste spirit, or desire to be chaste, or at least are willing to consider whether you should be. For there are some people so unclean they can take the most prudent speech and turn it into filthy talk. They study carnal sins, not to avoid them, but to learn ways to offend God and pollute their spirits. They search their houses with bright light to be instructed in all the corners of nastiness. I have tried in the following section to minister help to those who need it, but without causing impure thoughts. If anyone will snatch this pure candle from my hands and hold it up for devilish light, he will only burn his own fingers. I have tried to express these things purely and have cautioned readers how to read them.

Chastity is the duty symbolized by God in circumcision. It is circumcision of the heart, suppression of all irregular desires in matters of sexual pleasure. I call all desires irregular and sinful that are not sanctified by being (1) within marriage, (2) within natural order, and (3) within the moderation of Christian modesty. Sins against the first are fornication and adultery. Incest and homosexual acts violate the second. Against the third is unreasonable use of wedded sex. Concerning this last, judgment has to be made as with food and drink. One cannot specify a certain degree of frequency or mode for all people. But sex is to be ruled as all a person's other actions, with personal dignity and Christian honor.

Chastity keeps body and soul pure as God made them, whether single or married. Our duty is described by Paul in this way: "It is God's will that you should be sanctified: that you should avoid sexual immorality; that each of you should learn to control his own body in a way that is holy and honorable, not in passionate lust like the heathen, who do not know God" (1 Thess. 4:3–5 NIV).

Virginity is not in itself a state more acceptable to God; but voluntary virginity for religious purposes is better than married life. Not that it is more holy—but it provides a freedom from worldly cares, an opportunity to spend more time in spiritual employment. It does not attend as much on lower affairs. And those who have chosen singleness undergo greater self-denial.

Of course, it is possible for a married person to please God even more than most virgins. Married people can be examples of affection, they can be patient and contented, and they can educate children about God. Married or virgin or widowed, all can be servants of God and heirs of Jesus.

A chaste person resists all impure thoughts. He does not take pleasure in remembering past impurities. A chaste person does not have imaginary lovers or entertain his mind with secret desires.

A chaste person speaks purely, avoiding filthy language. He disapproves involuntary thoughts of evil. An involuntary thought is not sinful. But if a man takes pleasure in the involuntary thought and continues it, he is then choosing what was originally an accident and making the innocent sinful.

## Matrimonial Chastity

Although expressions of love are part of marriage, spouses must be spiritually as though they were not married. That is, while they love each other more than anyone else in the world, they must love God even more. Their mutual love must never cause them to slight God or to sin.

Regarding sex, they should consider God's intentions for that act. It is a vile husband who uses his wife as one would a prostitute, strictly for self-gratification. Sex is a desire to be satisfied, and fulfilling that desire brings personal pleasure, but that pleasure should always be joined with at least one of God's other intentions for sex. God has planned sex to meet a variety of purposes: It enables us to have children, avoid fornication, ease household tensions, lighten sorrow, express affection, and become more intimate. Sex can become a sacred act when accompanied by one of these ends.

## Remedies for Lust

1. When a temptation to lust strikes you, do not resist by considering the difficulties of getting away with it. Fly from that thought! If you try to imagine some of the problems involved, you'll soon be imagining the act itself. Even to consider whether you should engage in sex whets your appetite for it. A man with tar on his clothing shouldn't try to pull it off if he wants clean fingers.
2. Avoid idleness. Fill up your time with useful exertions, for lust usually creeps in during those

times when the mind and body are not occupied. Hard work, while it lasts, is the strongest defense against lust. A healthy person who just lies around the house can hardly expect to keep a chaste mind and body.

3. Avoid occasions of temptation: regular meetings in private with members of the opposite sex, indecent dancing, conversations about sexual escapades. Some of these are almost invitations to lust. Even the ones that seem innocent can be like mushrooms to inexperienced tasters; the poisonous ones are hard to recognize.

4. The greatest temptations usually come from people toward whom you feel affection. It is easy not to be tempted by rudeness or threats; but tenderness is hard to resist. A person will more quickly lay aside his coat for the warm sun than the bitter wind.

5. Pray earnestly to the king of purity, Christ the virgin, asking Him to cast out unclean thoughts. Prayer can restrain lust because prayer against it makes us less willing to give in.

6. Naturally, a final helpful remedy for lust is marriage.

# Chapter 7
*Humility*

Humility is the great jewel of the Christian religion, the ornament that distinguishes Christianity from all worldly wisdom. It is not taught by contemporary wisdom, but was both taught and exemplified by Jesus Christ. "Take my yoke upon you and learn from me, for I am gentle and humble in heart" (Matt. 11:29 NIV).

Everything that happens to us can be studied to further humility. Intelligence is no basis for pride. Even the most brilliant scholar has a thousand areas of ignorance for each sphere of knowledge in which he is competent. A learned person is basically one who makes more guesses than other people. That is hardly a thing to be proud of.

A person proud of having wealth is a fool. If he thinks he is better than others because he is worth more, let him think how inferior he is to a gold mine!

You have no reason to be proud of being spiritually superior to your neighbors. If you are better in a certain way, that is a gift from God—a better natural disposition or upbringing, better health, better spiritual instruction. For any of these advantages you owe praise to God, for you are indebted to Him. What person would take pride in being more deeply in debt than another?

*Acts of Humility*

1. Humility does not consist of tearing yourself
   down or wearing ragged clothes or going about
   with a servile posture. It means truly recognizing your own unworthiness before God. When
   we are sick or hungry, we genuinely believe it
   and freely admit it. The same should be true of
   our worthiness.
2. Whatever bad things you say about yourself, be
   contented that others should think the same. If
   you call yourself stupid, don't get mad if someone else agrees! After all, we all want others to
   agree with our real opinions. A person who says
   bad things about himself without really wanting
   them to be believed is a hypocrite, or is fishing
   for compliments.
3. Love to be concealed. Don't trouble yourself
   about being undervalued; be content if praise
   fails to come.
4. Never be ashamed of your background or your
   job. If someone asks about your job, and you
   are unemployed, admit it with the same freedom that you would tell of a status occupation.
5. Never speak anything of your activities simply
   to be noticed or commended. Of course, if
   relating what you have done will glorify God, or
   edify someone, or do anything else useful, you
   need not omit it for fear of having praise come
   your way. If it is important to tell someone of a
   good deed you've done, tell it. Just make sure
   that praise is not your real goal.
6. When you are praised for saying or doing
   something, accept it calmly. Reflect the praise to
   God as the giver of your gift or the blesser of

your action or the fulfiller of your plans. And thank God for enabling you to glorify Him.

7. Live righteously and get a good reputation for it. But let others comment on your reputation; don't dwell on it yourself.

8. Do not use subtle conversational devices to get praise. Some people put themselves down, thus managing to get others to comfort them regarding their good points. Others lead the conversation toward activities in which they have participated successfully. These people make their own bait to persuade themselves to swallow the hook.

9. Never waste time wishing people knew more about how much you accomplish or thinking about how impressed they'd be if they knew "the real you."

10. Let others be praised in your presence. Do not put down people being talked about, but encourage positive recognition of them.

11. Be content when others are selected for honor, and you are not; when their ideas are used, and yours are not; when they are given any preference at all over you.

12. Don't be eager to excuse your faults. If you do something wrong, admit it. Trying to cover up a sin is as useless as trying to hide a toothache by wearing cosmetics. And if someone accuses you falsely, don't become anxious worrying about who might have heard.

13. Thank God for your physical weaknesses and imperfections, which can be used as tools to learn humility. Thus wrote the apostle Paul about his affliction: "Three times I pleaded with the Lord to take it away from me. But he said to

me, 'My grace is sufficient for you, for my power is made perfect in weakness.' Therefore I will boast all the more gladly about my weaknesses, so that Christ's power may rest on me. That is why, for Christ's sake, I delight in weaknesses" (2 Cor. 12:8–10 NIV).

14. Do not chide another person's moral weakness just to irritate him. Do not report it to lessen his reputation. Do not reflect on it just to remind yourself how you are unlike him.

Humility is like every other grace; its beginning is a gift, and it grows through repetition.

*Means of Increasing Humility*

1. Confess your sins often to God. Our lives seem pretty good because our sins are scattered; yet if the sins of our entire lifetime were placed on a list before us, we would feel embarrassed and humbled.

2. Pray often for mercy.

3. Avoid efforts to move up in status. Be careful of the old pretense, "I want this bigger salary because I can do more good for others." Perhaps it will do more good for others. But the question is, will it do good for you? God is glorified as much by your contentment with a small salary as your generosity with a large one.

4. Meditate on the effects of pride and humility. "He mocks proud mockers but gives grace to the humble" (Prov. 3:34 NIV).

5. Remember the example of Jesus. His whole life was a continuous example of humility: a vast descent from the glories of heaven to the form of

a servant, a life of labor, a state of poverty, a cruel death. If Christ was humble in the midst of perfect wisdom and virtue, surely we should be humble with our imperfections.

6. If someone knocks on your door, do not suddenly change the activity you are engaged in unless modesty should require it. If you were asleep or playing or watching TV, do not snatch up a book to seem studious or a Bible to seem devout. It is a sign of pride to want to appear more studious or devout than we really are.

7. Choose some mature Christian with whom you can share your actions and thoughts. We become doubly careful to avoid faults that another human being will know about.

*Signs of Humility*

These fruits indicate a person rooted in humility:

1. The humble person does not trust simply in his own judgment but relies on friends, counselors, and spiritual guides.

2. He does not stubbornly pursue his own will but lets God choose for him in everything, and accepts the choices of his superiors in matters that concern them.

3. He does not gripe about requirements.

4. He bears injuries patiently.

5. He is not complacent about his conduct.

6. He loves to be with wise men, he praises good men, and he rips apart no one.

7. He recognizes that God may judge his actions differently than people do.

8. He is grateful for criticism and corrects faults.

9. He is willing to do good to those who stab him in the back, just as Christ washed the feet of Judas.

# Chapter 8
*Decorum*


Decorum is an appendage of self-control. It is to chastity and humility what fringe is to a garment. Decorum serves to moderate curiosity and arrogance.

*The Practice of Decorum*

1. Do not keep trying to figure out why God does things, but be content to learn your duty. God's commandments are proclaimed to everyone; God's plans are kept to Himself.
2. Do not inquire into affairs that are none of your business.
3. Do not eavesdrop, which breaks your neighbor's privacy. If someone says he is having a personal problem, don't ask what it is; he just said it was personal.

Each person has sufficient personal material in endeavoring to know himself. What difference does it make now whether your neighbor's first child was illegitimate? What does it help to know that one church member has a sexual problem or another spends money too freely?

The inquisitive (busybodies, Paul calls them) are not chiefly curious about righteous lives or well-run families. (That is, their curiosity has no benevolent motivation.) They want to hear about arguments and failings and hidden problems.

There are certainly enough things yet to discover. How are stars formed? How can food production be increased? But these problems aren't enough to occupy the minds of busybodies! They want to feed on intimate tragedies and bad news, which plainly shows the touch of evil.

If a doctor went from house to house unsent for and asked what secret diseases were in the house, he would be unwelcome even if he said he could help cure them. Knock on the door before you enter the privacy of your neighbor's heart.

### Acts of Decorum

1. Do not answer a question asked of someone else.
2. Do not confidently relay information about which you are unsure. Report things according to the degree of certainty you actually possess.
3. Do not pretend to know more than you really do, but freely admit areas of ignorance.
4. Act appropriately to the occasion. Don't be a wet blanket at a party or create laughter at a funeral home. "Rejoice with those who rejoice; mourn with those who mourn" (Rom. 12:15 NIV).
5. Do not jeer at others or make fun of them cuttingly.
6. It is against decorum for a woman to marry a second husband while still pregnant from the first, and she should not go out with anyone while her cheeks are still wet with funeral tears.
7. Wear modest and decent clothing. Don't pretend

to hide your nakedness with cloth so thin that it can be vaguely seen through. That kind of allurement sets a snare for a soul.

8. Let those who work well under you know that you are pleased with their diligence and good conduct.

9. Do not walk in a seductive manner, which God condemns by his prophets: "The women of Zion are haughty, walking along with out-stretched necks, flirting with their eyes, tripping along with mincing steps, with ornaments jingling on their ankles" (Isa. 3:16 NIV).

10. Avoid expensive cosmetics and dresses. Paul expressly directed this to Christian women: "I also want women to dress modestly, with decency and propriety, not with braided hair or gold or pearls or expensive clothes, but with good deeds, appropriate for women who profess to worship God" (1 Tim. 2:9–10 NIV).

11. As we should avoid tempting foods when we are not hungry, so we should decline going after spectacles that do not convert us—fires, auto accidents, and so on.

12. These may seem like little things. But I remind you of the words of the son of Sirach in the Apocrypha: "He who scourns small things will fall little by little" (Ecclus.19:1 [Apocrypha]).

# Chapter 9
*Faith*

IN one sense, the whole duty of man is worship. But in a more restricted sense, worship is that part of our duty particularly related to giving God honor. In it we admire His goodness, remark on His excellence, love His person, and believe His words.

Internal worship serves God by holding faith, hope, and love. Faith believes God's revelation, hope awaits His promises, and love delights in His excellence. Faith surrenders the understanding to God, hope surrenders earthly passions to heavenly affection, and love surrenders the will to God's service. Faith is opposed to unbelief, hope to despair, and love to hostility. These three together sanctify the whole person.

## What Is Faith?

1. Faith means to believe everything God has revealed to us. Once convinced that God has spoken, we are to make no further inquiry but to humbly submit, always remembering that there are some things we can never understand.

2. Faith is believing only those things that produce love for God. Whoever believes God to be cruel is evil. Whoever holds that God speaks one thing publicly but another thing privately is an enemy to faith. We must remove all imperfections from our conceptions of God.

3. Faith believes all God's promises, as surely as if we had them in our hands. Faith believes that in time of need God will do for us everything in His power. And His power is all-powerful.

4. Faith believes not only the promises but the duties. Many believe in the forgiveness of their sins, but they believe the doctrine without confirming it with repentance. They believe a different thing from what God intended. We are to trust God's covenant, and that covenant includes a response to His grace. God will be our God as long as we will be His people. To believe otherwise is not faith but sheer optimism, wishful thinking.

5. To have faith is to profess publicly Jesus Christ and to follow His commands openly— unashamed of God's Word.

6. Faith prays without doubting or hopelessness, not suspicious of God but confident that God's answer, whatever it is, will be gracious and merciful.

These acts of faith are the servants of Jesus in any stage of growth. Some have faith as a grain of mustard seed; some grow up to a sprout; some have faith as a tree. But even the smallest faith requires action on what we believe.

*Signs of True Faith*

1. A key sign is earnest, fervent prayer. It would be incredible for us to truly believe the wonderful offers of God and not desire them of Him.
2. Faith is content with God as our Judge, our Benefactor, our Master, and our Friend. Faith wants for God to mean as much to us as we do to Him.
3. Faith turns all our principal desires from earth to heaven. Suppose a beggar knew himself secretly to be heir to a king in another land, with his coronation to take place shortly. How his thoughts would keep jumping to the future! He would eagerly anticipate entering his kingdom. God has made us co-heirs with Jesus Christ. If we believed this, it would continually affect our thoughts and emotions. But a person who thinks only about making more money or grows distressed at losing it—either that person has no riches in heaven or else he doesn't really believe he does.
4. James' sign of faith is the surest: "I will show you my faith by what I do" (James 2:18 NIV). Because King Ferdinand of Aragon believed the story Columbus told, he furnished Columbus with ships. Ferdinand got the West Indies by his active faith. Henry VII of England also believed, but not enough to provide Columbus with a ship; Henry's faith brought nothing.
5. A believer does not fret but waits patiently until times of refreshment come. He is no more nervous about next year than about last year. A man lacks faith who is only confident about his needs being met when he has a large savings account.

*Ways to Obtain Faith*

1. Have a humble, willing mind that desires to be instructed in God's ways. Faith enters like a sunbeam. Simply draw back the curtain and the Son of righteousness will enlighten your darkness.

2. Avoid curiosity about mysteries and about who causes different circumstances. True faith trusts without prying into indiscernible matters. A farmer does not carry his bed into his field to observe personally how each ear of corn grows; he tends the general field and trusts that the crop will be produced.

3. Do not study Christian evidence only when doubts come. Consider the evidence when you are mentally and physically healthy so that you may have confidence when hard times arrive.

# Chapter 10
## *Hope*

While faith concerns the good and evil that occur to everyone, hope is only about the good that is offered to us. We hope about things that are less certain than faith, because they are offered on conditions that we may choose not to accept. For instance, I can have faith that there is a heaven for the godly in Christ Jesus, including myself, if I continue in Christ. But that I personally shall enter heaven is the object of my hope, not my faith; it is only a certainty as I choose to continue in Christ.

*Hope*

1. Hope confidently relies upon God's promises.
2. Hope recognizes that problems and troubles are not defects in God's plan. They are due either to a fault of ours or a decision of His.
3. Hope rejoices in the midst of sorrow, knowing that this can work for good, and will if we love God. Hope looks through the cloud for a beam of light from God. This is rejoicing in tribulation; every degree of hope brings a degree of joy.
4. Hope desires and prays and longs for the object

of our hope, the pearl of great price. And it desires the things of this life to the degree that they glorify God and help people. Hope sends our prayers soaring up to heaven. Without hope it is impossible to pray, but hope makes our prayers reasonable and fervent.

5. Perseverance is the culmination of hope. We continue in our duties only as long as we have hope. A person who is told to build a whole castle in an hour will sit down and not even bother to begin.

6. Let your hope be patient, without tediousness of spirit or the presumption of prescribing a time. Set no limits or requirements on God; but let your prayers and endeavors go on with patient waiting for God's timing. The men of Bethulia resolved to wait upon God only five more days, which was presumptuous.*

*Taylor is referring to the eighth chapter of Judith in the Apocrypha. The rulers of Bethulia, besieged by the Assyrians for thirty-four days, met together and vowed that if God did not deliver their city in five more days, they would give up hope in him and surrender. Judith, a devout widow of the town, chided their action. Since most Protestant readers will not have ready access to this significant passage, and Judith's speech to the rulers of Bethulia is the key to Taylor's sixth point, I include it here:

"Who are you to tempt the Lord? This is not a promise that may draw down mercy, but rather that may stir up wrath, and enkindle indignation. You have set a limit to the mercy of the Lord, and you have told him to act as it pleases you. But since the Lord acts in his own good time, let us be patient as he is and with many tears let us beg his pardon. God is not like man, nor can he be threatened like a human being. Therefore, let us humble our souls before him and in a humble spirit

175

7. Do not take every trouble as a reason to despair, but continue hoping. And if any misfortune interrupts your work, simply come back to it again.

The main causes of despair are faintheartedness and self-centeredness. A selfish person can't stand delay and grows desperate when things aren't going his way.

*Remedies for Despair*

1. Be indifferent to circumstances and the hopes of the world. A person who imagines to himself thousands of little hopes that depend (as they always do in this world) on ten thousand circumstances will often find events falling short of his expectations and be downhearted.
2. Remember the scriptural attributes of God. He is strong, wise, and true—and He loves you.
3. God has promised that even denials and losses will work for good to those who love Him.
4. Think about this: God can do for us whatever He pleases. Being infinitely loving, He desires always to do what's best for us; being infinitely wise, He knows what that best is. This thought, in every period of history, has supported the afflicted people of God and carried them on dry ground through their Red Seas.
5. Are you tempted to despair of your salvation? Consider how much Christ suffered to redeem you from your sins. If you really think about this, God's desire to save you is boundless; He will not be easily satisfied without saving you.

---

continue in his service. Let us ask the Lord with tears to show us mercy if that be his will" (Jth 8:11–17).

6. Let no one despair of God's forgiveness, unless he can prove that his sins are greater than God's mercy—which, for a repentant person who is within God's covenant, cannot be.
7. Remember times in the past when you have experienced God and sensed His presence. This serves as an anchor against the fluctuating emotions of the present.

If circumstances go against you, destroying your earthly confidence, you can always retire to the castle of grace. The more you are defeated on this earth, the more hope you will place elsewhere.

# Chapter 11
*Love*

L ove is the greatest thing God can give us, for He is love; and it is the greatest thing we can give back to Him. It is the greatest commandment and the fulfiller of all the commandments. God's goodness to us and our emotional experiences of His presence first draw us to Him. But once we have tasted God's goodness, we love Him simply for His goodness (not necessarily to us). Thanking becomes adoring, and we desire union with God.

There are only two qualities that create true love—perfection and fulfillment. We admire and desire as we sense objects or people approaching these qualities. Yet the ultimate perfection and fulfillment can be found only in God.

*Acts of Love to God*

When it is inquired whether a person is a good man, the meaning of the question is not "What does he believe?" or "What does he hope for?" but "What does he love?"

1. Love does the things that please the Beloved; it keeps His commandments. "This is love for

God: to obey his commands" (1 John 5:3 NIV).
Love is obedient.

2. Love looks not only for direct commands but
   also for subtle ways to please. It continually
   seeks out new avenues of expressing itself.

3. Love advances the interests of the Beloved. For
   example, it spends money in the ways He would
   spend it if He were here.

4. Love is impatient with things that may displease
   the Beloved. It hates sin as the enemy of its
   friend. Love marries into the family; it takes on
   the same friendships and hatreds.

5. Love forever wants to be around, to talk with, to
   enjoy its Beloved. It loves to talk about Him, tell
   His stories, and repeat His words. Every degree
   of imitation and union is a degree of love. Love
   can endure anything except the Beloved's displeasure or absence.

God is not to be used like cologne, which we enjoy
when we have it but can easily live without. True love is
restless when it is not around God. The desire for God is
a hunger that must be fed.

6. When circumstances change, love looks at the
   Beloved to gauge His reaction. A person who
   loves the Lord is satisfied for God to distribute
   His gifts wherever He wills.

7. Love is eager to learn when God is the Teacher,
   and it is content to remain ignorant (and silent)
   about what God has not chosen to reveal.

8. Love wants to behave like an angel, even a
   seraph, for the Beloved. It aims beyond its
   reach.

Love is constant. It is not a tide that ebbs and flows but an ever-growing river.

9. Ask God to change your desires. It is hard for a person to choose what he does not like. Converse with God by frequent prayer, and desire right desires.
10. Lay out all your needs before God; it is natural to love the One who keeps us going. Call to Him for health; run to Him for counseling.

Love wants God to be obeyed. Martyrdom is an instance of obedient love, for it witnesses to a readiness of mind to suffer any evil rather than to do any.

Zeal for the Lord's cause is a mark of love—but it must be controlled. Zeal should spend its greatest heat in those things that concern ourselves; it should be re-strained in things that concern others. Fervency is safer in personal deportment than in counseling.

Paul's zeal was expressed in preaching without any salary, in traveling, in spending and being spent for his flock, in suffering, in being willing to accept curses for the sake of the gospel. Our zeal should be as his was: great in affections toward others, not in anger against them. The first is never dangerous, the second seldom safe. If your zeal must be expressed in severity, be severe toward yourself.

# Chapter 12
## *Charity*

Real charity is as busy and active as fire. But it must be accompanied by love; charity without love is like a prayer without devotion. Charity involves a prompt, noble mind, making us eager to do helpful things for those in need (or even out of need).

Charity is one of God's means to reduce the inequality of possessions natural to a fallen world. There are two kinds of charity, physical and spiritual, and several ways of expressing each. Physical charity includes what Jesus taught: feeding the hungry, providing clothes for the poor, visiting the sick, and welcoming strangers. Other expressions of physical charity are: taking sick people to the doctor, making sure the homes of the poor are heated, providing aids for the blind, loaning money, finding jobs for the unemployed, and providing workers with good tools.

Spiritual charity includes teaching, counseling, comforting, admonishing, forgiving, and praying for others. Also, it involves gentleness in correction and encouragement.

A person who provides charity should do it for the sake of mercy—that is, he should attempt to understand and sympathize with his brother's calamity. Charity should be perceived as an attempt to ease ourselves and our brothers out of a common misfortune.

A person who gives charity must not do it for the purpose of being noticed. To this end, the person who has done a good deed should generally forget it and never mention it again.

Give to Christians rather than non-Christians, when the needs are equal. If fact, even if the unbelievers' needs are somewhat greater, give primarily to the Christian community. But if an unbeliever is in desperate straits, while the believer can survive without help, then by all means assist the unbeliever. If the believer is a real Christian, he would want you to do that anyway.

Do not give charity to people who will use it to support their sin, such as drunkenness or continuing idleness. The apostle Paul warned the church at Thessalonica about idle loafers: "We gave you this rule: 'If a man will not work, he shall not eat' " (2 Thess. 3:10 NIV).

Search into the needs of humble families, for there are many people who have nothing left except misery and modesty. We must work extra hard to discover their needs and then convey relief in a manner that will not make them feel shame.

Give without expecting any return. Give to children, the ungrateful, the dying, and those you may never see again. Giving with a desire to receive back, whether money or even gratitude, is not charity but an investment.

Give even to your enemies. You may win them to yourself, but don't make that your goal. Let your intention be simply to do good and to win them for God.

Do not merely give money to organizations and consider charity fulfilled. Visit the inner-city ministries yourself. Invite furloughed missionaries to your home. When your eye sees what it has never seen before, then your mind will think new thoughts. You will find your heart made tender as you come to know personally the needs of the poor, and your hand's giving will follow your heart's prompting.

There are several ways to improve in charity. One is to determine, when entering a contest or sweepstakes, to give away whatever you might win to the poor. People who enter lotteries can do the same thing. Of course, it would be even wiser to leave the game alone; take the money spent on lottery tickets and other contests and give *that* to the poor.

Another way to grow in charity is to fast. Fasting is not commanded in the New Testament, but it is useful self-denial. The meal money saved can be given to the poor. After all, if we are not willing to go without food occasionally to make sure a brother can eat, we would hardly be willing to die for him.

Direct your continual thoughts of how to make money into a different channel: how to help others more effectively. Why should we not do as much for charity as for greed, as much for heaven as for the fading world, as much for God and Jesus as for comfort and entertainment?

When you have no money to contribute, have mercy. Pray for the poor. If you do what you can, physical or spiritual, money or prayer, it will be accepted. We are to give what we have, not what we lack. Charity gives what it can; and when it cannot relieve a burden, it feels sorrow.

# Chapter 13
*The Word of God*

The Word of God is recorded in the Bible. We can know nothing else to be His message for certain. Good books and sermons are only the words of men, yet good teaching is important to Christianity. After all, the person who preaches an hour against drunkenness has been conveying God's Word "Do not get drunk on wine" (Eph. 5:18 NIV). And a person who writes a book helps the people who read it even more than one who preaches a sermon on the subject.

Still, the Holy Spirit is the best preacher in the world, and the words of Scripture are the best sermons. Everything necessary for salvation is set down there.

*Profiting from God's Word*

1. Set aside a portion of your time specifically for Scripture study.
2. Spend most of your study time on those parts about Christ and our following of Him—that is, on the Gospels and Epistles.
3. Listen attentively to Scripture readings in worship services.

4. Before reading Scripture, pray for willingness to learn. Ask God to write the words in your heart and help you portray them in your life.

*Profiting from Sermons and Christian Books*

1. When reading or listening, be diligent to hear. Don't entertain worldly cares. Make efforts to remember and plans to practice the good things you learn.
2. If you dislike the preacher or author, don't let that keep you from learning good things he may say.
3. Ask spiritually mature people what Christian books they recommend; it will be well worth the time you spend.

*A Prayer before Reading Scripture*

Holy and eternal God, let Your Holy Spirit rest on me while I read Your Word. Let me do it humbly, reverently, and without prejudiced views. Give me a mind eager not only to learn but to obey, that I may glorify the holy name of Jesus. Amen.

# Chapter 14
*Prayer*

Prayer is the greatest means in the world for showing to us our sinful nature and natural inclinations away from Christianity. Everyone is at least occasionally reluctant to pray, and most Christians are virtually always reluctant to pray. We're not able to pray very long at a time, and our minds teem with things to do rather than take an opportunity to pray.

Yet what is the tiresome thing we avoid? It is simply desiring God to give us His greatest gifts, the things that will make us truly happy. It is uplifting, physically easy as duties go, and not at all unpleasant. Except for the incarnation of Christ, there is no aspect of Christianity that better shows God's desire to save us and our unwillingness to accept. The fact that we neglect such an easy duty that God rewards so greatly is the ultimate testimony to His goodness and our carelessness.

Prayer is desiring of things worthy to be desired. It is our attempt to express that desire to God. Our reluctance to pray indicates that our longings for God are not as strong as we usually think they are.

*Practicing Prayer*

1. Let us principally ask God for the ability to glorify Him. He wants us to ask this and He delights to answer it.

2. We may lawfully pray to God for spiritual gifts that minister to the church—teaching ability, the gift of prayer, wisdom and opportunities to use it. But we must be careful that we are seeking only God's glory. And we must submit to God's will, allowing Him to furnish what He knows we need.

3. We may pray for necessities, which God has promised to provide. And even things that are not actual needs we may pray for, provided we do it with submission to God's will and without impatience.

4. All prayers should be made with faith and hope. We must believe we will receive what God wants us to ask, and we must hope for the things He has permitted us to ask. Our hope will not be in vain, even if we miss something not promised; for we can expect to find as great a blessing in the denial as in the granting.

5. Our prayers for what God has commanded should be intense and earnest. Our prayers for spiritual help should not be less fervent than our prayers for physical help.

6. Our prayers need not be wordy, merely sufficient to express our desires. God does not listen to us for many words but for earnest desire. Prayers are not measured by length but by love.

7. Mingle thanksgiving with your requests. This is Paul's advice: "Do not be anxious about

anything, but in everything, by prayer and peti-
tion, with thanksgiving, present your requests to
God" (Phil. 4:6 NIV).

8. Whatever we ask of God, let us also work
toward it if there is anything we can do. God
blesses effort, but He has no desire to support
idleness. Therefore, Jesus in His teaching joins
watchfulness with prayer. Read Scripture; then
pray to God for understanding. Pray against
temptation, but also "resist the devil, and he
will flee from you" (James 4:7 NIV). Ask God
to supply your physical needs; but if you want
to see those needs supplied, work for them. We
work, we pray for blessing, and we leave the
outcome to God—without worrying.

9. Let your posture express your prayer—sometimes kneeling, sometimes lifting hands to
heaven, sometimes lying face down. But we may
pray anywhere, even on a city street, and under
any circumstances. It is well to do so. Those of
us employed full-time cannot pray as often as
we'd like unless we are willing to do it under less
than ideal conditions.

One of our chief difficulties in prayer is wandering
thoughts. To combat this we can use prayer to be assisted
in prayer. Pray for your thoughts to be continually pulled
back on target. Also, you can use Scripture prayers and
other written prayers to focus your mind.

A key thing we can do to control wandering minds is
to avoid multiple businesses in the world. In necessary
business, labor for tranquility of spirit. Be calm in the tempests of fortune. We can pay better attention to Christianity when we are not torn in pieces with the cares of the
world.

It is almost irreverent to desire God to hear prayers that we have not listened to ourselves. If they are not worthy of our attention, why should we consider them worthy of God's?

The other great problem in prayer is a sense of tediousness. The Jews grew tired of worship saying, "When will the New Moon be over that we may sell grain, and the Sabbath be ended that we may market wheat?" (Amos 8:5 NIV).

Many Christians are equally weary of being called to worship. They pray dully. They seldom meditate, seldom examine themselves, and seldom go deeper into Christianity than determining what they "have to do." Material things are their comfort in misfortune. They do not seek counsel from mature Christians but follow their own judgment, which follows their desires, which follow worldly pleasure. When the Spirit puts within them an inclination to extra virtue, they put the inclination back out. In short, these people are tired of Christianity, and they want to sit at the very foot of the mount of the Lord, not near the Lord Himself.

Our prayers can be made less tedious with variety—singing a hymn, for instance. But do not feel emotional "highs" are a requirement of prayer. Early in the Christian life God often encourages our weak spirits with overflowings of joy and pleasure that we can almost feel. And He continues this, on a less frequent basis, all our lives. Yet this is not always a good thing for us to have, and it is not safe to seek after. It is running after Christ not for Himself but for His loaves and fish—not a desire to be pleasing to God, but to be pleased ourselves. Our devotions are not useless when we fail to "feel" anything, nor are they necessarily better when we do.

# Prayers

### For Ourselves

Gracious Father, have mercy on Your servant; I bow my head and knees and heart to You. Forgive my sins, and give me grace to repent. Strengthen me with Your Holy Spirit that I may fulfill my calling. Keep me ever in true Christian faith and in love of You and my neighbors.

Holy Jesus, preserve Your spouse, whom You have redeemed and cleansed with Your blood. We are founded on a rock but planted in a stormy sea. Preserve us from splitting apart. Amen.

### For Ministers

Jesus, Great Shepherd and Bishop of our souls, give Your pastor-servant a spirit of faith, love, and diligence. Let him declare Your will to the people faithfully. Combine in him a holy life and true belief, to Your glory. Amen.

### For Family

Merciful God, let Your compassion rest upon my family. Please give them healthy bodies and spirits. Let us all be united to the Lord Jesus with bands of love, becoming a holy family. Being Your adopted grace-children in this life, let us be part of Your heavenly family forever.

Almighty God, fill all Your people with love and devotion. We long for You and await a joyful resurrection through Jesus Christ. Amen.

# Chapter 15
*The Brevity of Life*

Man is a bubble, says a Greek proverb. And indeed we are fragile. Homer calls us a leaf, Pindar terms us the dream of a shadow, and James describes us as a vapor. There are so many ways to die that staying alive is as much a miracle as being created in the first place. We take pains to accumulate goods to keep us alive, and our very exertions build up stress that pushes us down the road to death. We die, and the goods we bought to sustain us remain behind.

I have talked with some folks who rejoiced in the deaths of their enemies and called it a judgment. But months later those same people faced even harder death. When I saw this, I cried. Our quarrels with each other all end by being sent to a final Judge, God.

It is remarkable how frugal God is with time. He has scattered the sky with stars like a gardener scattering grass seed over a lawn. He has made an incredible variety of animals. He has provided us a wide choice of food and drink, even though a very few would have kept us alive. Yet God parcels out time carefully, drop by drop. We never have several minutes together to choose from, but one minute leaves as God provides the next. This should teach us to value our time; God's scanty distribution of it indicates the worth of each moment.

Yes, life is short. But life contains so many miseries that we are fortunate it is short. God, in pity to mankind, abbreviates our state of misery; otherwise the burden of life would be well-nigh unbearable. People in the greatest pain have generally the shortest time to live.

We, perhaps, may be prosperous. But have you considered how few of the world's people are? Oppressed people fill all corners of the earth with groans and fill heaven itself with weeping prayers.

Death is not terrifying to people such as these. Most of us shrink at the thought of having a wisdom tooth pulled. But if that tooth becomes infected and causes continual pain, we are eager to have it pulled. We expect relief from the pulling. Death is not terrifying to those who feel the pain of this life and have hope of something better.

# Chapter 16
*Patience in Illness*

The death that God visited upon Adam (and upon us, his descendants) was not simply going out of this world, but the manner of going. If Adam had stayed innocent, he could have left this world calmly and happily; he would not have died in sickness or pain. But when he fell, he began to die that very day, according to God. In other words, on that day he began to degenerate. Mankind became susceptible to disease and, therefore, death.

But Christ repaired the world when He suffered and overcame death for us. He has taken away the sting of death and the dishonor of dissolution. We can now be reconciled to sickness. As it came in by sin, it loses power in the presence of Christ.

The first great temptation of illness is impatience. Usually the sick are exhorted to patience by those who are well and do not fully understand. We need to recognize what type of patience a sick person can actually have.

Groans, pleading prayers, and agonized faces are the language of the sick. It is inappropriate to expect a person in pain to take on the role of an actor and pretend all is well. It would be well, of course, if those in pain *could* regulate their faces in a way not to cause distress to those with them. But this doesn't really help the sick person in his fight against impatience.

Silence and a cheerful look are not part of a sick man's duty; "I am worn out calling for help," says David (Ps. 69:3 NIV). And Hezekiah, in describing his illness, said, "I moaned like a mourning dove" (Isa. 38:14 NIV). That is the fitting voice of sickness. It is not the cry of sinful impatience, but a plea for pity.

Some people are so physically sensitive that the same load is double to them what it would be to someone else. Therefore, we cannot judge the patience of someone who groans more than others do in that illness. Some people are naturally tender, and others are tough. Even Jesus, as His suffering peaked on the cross, cried out with a loud voice. Our Savior was not guilty of impatience.

To be innocent, our groans and crying must be without despair. Despair sins against God's known reputation for goodness and against our previous help from Him. Despair makes pain intolerable. (Despair—the complete loss of hope—is a chief element of hell.)

Against despair we should exercise hope. We show that we hope by praying to God for help and comfort.

Our anguish in illness should also be without peevishness. We may groan, but not in a way that magnifies our sorrows or causes trouble for those trying to help us. Patience in this regard means following doctors' orders, doing what we can (even if unpleasant) to get well, and being gentle with those who take care of us. When our friends and nurses make mistakes, we should not explode in angry words or rage within.

Serious illness is the greatest human calamity. We should not lightly judge a person's patience by his tossing from side to aside and the plaintive tone of voice. A person is patient who calls upon God, who hopes to receive either health or heaven, who believes God can afflict him and still be just, who expects God to use the illness for a good purpose, and who is gentle with those around him.

Those who patiently submit to God's will regarding illness can even find advantages in it. Most of us have adult bodies and childish souls. But in sickness, as the body weakens, the soul often grows. People who are awake and in pain mark the hours with prayer.

Sickness alleviates pride. We spend less concern on preening and appearance. When our head aches, we don't realize how little our frequent and loud debates do for the soul. We lay aside everything that has brought us fame, all our confidence, and we care to know only Jesus Christ the crucified.

# Chapter 17
*Facing Illness as a Child of God*


God does nothing in vain. He offers us the message of the Scriptures and the Holy Spirit as a Comforter because He knows we will need them. The reason we are exhorted to patience in the first place is that God knows we are going to suffer.

When serious illness comes your way, do not let your thoughts run wild. Remember that this is an expected part of life. Remember that you are yet a child of God. When the sun is behind a cloud, it still shines.

Do not dwell on all the possible pains and dangers of your condition. A person in an airplane who looks down at the ground and thinks about how far that is to fall, how many seconds it would take, how hard the plane would hit, and how it might explode will create a longer and greater time of terror than he would experience if the plane actually did crash. A person who dwells on all the possible upcoming tests and operations and sleepless nights and expenses creates artificial diseases worse than the real one.

For comfort, pick some little saying from a book or sermon that has lifted you in the past and hold onto it tightly.

When you are weak, short thoughts are more effective than elaborately reasoned discourses.

Do not be afraid that because you can't "work for God"

now, you are falling out of His favor. Accept the fact that you can't read the Bible now if you must rest your eyes. Since God has chosen to allow your condition, it is foolish for you to become frustrated that you can't serve Him during this time. If He needed your service, He would enable it.

Do not think God is moved only by protracted prayers; He knows the effort of a sigh to him uttered during pain. In painful illness, place yourself in God's presence as often as possible. If you can do more, do it; but if you can't, don't let it be a source of impatience. When we cannot labor, we yet can love.

Again, treat gently nurses and others who serve you. Remember that you are causing them extra effort. It is not their desire to hurt you. They want you to be glad they are around. It is perverted justice for you to want them to be miserable just because you are. A person can hardly hope to be patient under the chastening of God who finds fault with the well-intentioned efforts of friends.

Do not, under the pain of your illness, cry out for death. Be prepared to die, but be equally prepared (which may be harder) to live. Accept the station where your General has placed you.

A person in agonizing illness can benefit from reading (or having read to him) the sixth, sixteenth, and thirty-first psalms. The last of those opens thus:

"In you, O LORD, I have taken refuge; let me never be put to shame; deliver me in your righteousness. Turn your ear to me, come quickly to my rescue; be my rock of refuge, a strong fortress to save me. Since you are my rock and my fortress, for the sake of your name lead me and guide me. Free me from the trap that is set for me, for you are my refuge. Into your hands I commit my spirit; redeem me, O LORD, the God of truth" (Ps. 31:1–5 NIV).

After the reading of one of these psalms the sick person may use the following prayer as a pattern for his own:

Almighty God, in Your justice You sent sickness and death into the world as a punishment for sin. You allowed suffering in the world—not to destroy us, but to show Your mercy toward us. Your justice ministers to Your mercy. This slight momentary trouble is producing for us an everlasting weight of glory (2 Cor. 4:17).

As You have turned sin into sickness, please turn my sickness into opportunities for holiness. You have called me to the fellowship of suffering. Let my suffering be united to the sufferings of my Lord. For His sake, pity and assist me. Relieve my sorrow; support my spirit. I know that You have the greatest amount of pity in the world.

Yet do with me as You please. Choose for me not only my overall condition, but any minor inconveniences that may accompany it.

Yet remember my weaknesses, and enable me to rejoice in You. This cross lies heavy upon my shoulders; the spirit is willing, but the flesh is weak. I humbly beg that You enable me to rejoice in this situation. I genuinely believe that You are the same God of grace when You allow pain as when You relieve my weakness.

Holy Jesus, I am unable to stand under this cross, unable of myself. Pity me; strengthen me; save and deliver me. You have felt this burden Yourself. You sank under it, and You permitted a man to bear part of the load You were carrying. Please bear part of my load now by fortifying my spirit, by being my strength when I am weak. Be the Christ who empowers me to face any situation (Phil. 4:13).

If You choose to support me, I will praise You; if You choose me to undergo yet heavier burdens, I will cry out to You. Strengthen the hands and hearts of those who are taking care of me. Let me pass through the valley of the shadow of death in safety, sensing Your mercy. Though I break in pieces, I hope for You to gather me up; grant this prayer for the sake of the Savior who suffered for me. Amen.

# Chapter 18
*Visiting the Sick*

Visitors to a sick person should pray for his health (while accepting God's will) and for his patience. They should not wait to come until the patient is dying, but before, that they may minister while he can understand.

The weaker a patient is, the less visitors should talk and the more they should pray. A person full of pain needs someone to talk to God for him. Prayers need not be long, but they need to be frequent, fervent, and holy. The patient may join in or listen as he feels like it.

Sometimes a dying patient will ask whether we think he is going to be saved or not. We cannot give a definite answer from another human being. But to devout Christians, we can minister the following comforts:

1. Christ came into the world to save sinners
   (1 Tim. 1:15).
2. God takes no pleasure in the death of a sinner
   (Ezek. 33:11).
3. Christ is a perpetual advocate interceding for
   our pardon.
4. God uses infinite opportunities to reconcile us
   to Himself.

5. Under the law, a covenant of obedience, God still gave pardon, even to those who had sinned greatly. He forgave David the adulterer, Manasseh the idol-builder, and the Israelites after a number of idolatries. The prophets continually preached God's mercy and pardon to those who would repent. If God, then, would not pardon us who repent now, the gospel would be harsher than the law.

6. Communion, by its repetition, signifies to us who partake that we continue at all times in the safety of Jesus' sacrifice.

7. Christ calls us to forgive our brother seventy times seven. Yet immediately afterward Christ contrasted that ample pardon with God's forgiveness by comparing it to forgiveness of a debt of twenty-five dollars as opposed to twenty million dollars (Matt. 18:21–27).

8. He who does not break a bruised reed or quench a dimly burning wick (Isa. 42:3) will not tie us to perfection for salvation. We do not have to be perfect in order to be saved.

9. It is almost unbelievable that God would take on human hands and feet. It is even more unbelievable that He allowed those hands and feet to be nailed to a cross. But impossibly unbelievable would it be for God to suffer like that, do so much for us, and yet allow those of us who long for what He made possible to miss it. God did not die for angels. We are His entire reason for becoming human and dying.

Eternal life is the gift of God (Rom. 6:23). Even if my sins were fewer, it would still be a gift. And God has set no boundaries on receiving this gift except that we be within His covenant, repentant people desiring to serve Him.

So comfort the patient and read to Him Psalm 130 (NIV), which follows:

> *Out of the depths I cry to you, O LORD; O LORD, hear my voice. Let your ears be attentive to my cry for mercy. If you, O LORD, kept a record of sins, O LORD, who could stand? But with you there is forgiveness; therefore you are feared.*
>
> *I wait for the LORD, my soul waits, and in his word I put my hope. My soul waits for the LORD more than watchmen wait for the morning, more than watchmen wait for the morning. O Israel, put your hope in the LORD, for with the LORD is unfailing love and with him is full redemption. He himself will redeem Israel from all their sins.*

# INTRODUCTION TO THE DEVOUT LIFE

## FRANCIS DE SALES

# FRANCIS DE SALES (1567–1622)

Francis was born to the House of Sales (hence his name) in France in 1567. He studied philosophy, rhetoric, law, and theology at French and Italian universities for several years, receiving his doctorate in law in 1591. Becoming ordained as a priest in 1593, Francis worked upward through church ranks, eventually being named a bishop. During the early 1600s, Francis wrote out occasional instructions on how to live effectively for God; these were published in 1609 as *Introduction to the Devout Life*. Francis died in 1622 and was declared a saint in 1665.

The *Introduction* became immediately popular throughout Europe; it was translated into Italian in 1610, English in 1613, and Spanish in 1618. In fact, fifty years after publication it was already found in seventeen different languages! Part of its appeal was that, at a time when Protestants and Catholics continually warred (both verbally and physically) over theological matters, Francis's book focused on how to love God effectively. That appeal has continued to the present day.

# A Note to the Reader

Dear Reader: Please read this foreword, and both of us will be satisfied.

A Greek flower-seller named Glycera knew so well how to arrange flowers that with the same set of blooms she could make an almost limitless number of bouquets. The Holy Spirit exercises the same type of skill when He presents lessons on devotion. The teaching is always the same; but the tongues and pens of devout servants can present it in a variety of beautiful ways. Regarding devotion, all I can write is what has already been said; indeed, that's all I want to write. Reader, I am presenting to you familiar flowers, but a new bouquet.

Most of the great devotional writers have traditionally assumed their audience to be pastors, nuns, and other people a step removed from the world. I am writing for politicians, businesspeople, homemakers—people who appear to live an "ordinary life." I want to show them that a saint can live in the world without being tainted by it. Yes, it's hard—that's why I want to see more people making an all-out effort at it. And, feeble as I am, I want to try to help.

This book was originally a series of notes written to a friend who wanted to lead a devout life. She passed them on to a professor, who urged their publication. To make the notes useful in a book for the public, I revised and put them into a semblance of order. But I have done this with hardly any spare time. What you have here is no theology textbook, but simply a collection of teachings given in good faith. I write in plain and simple words. (At least that's what I wanted to do.) As far as fancying up the language and really impressing you with my style—well, I have plenty of other things to do.

Finally, Reader, I admit that I write about the devout life without being perfectly devout myself. But I really wish I were devout, and this gives me the courage to try to teach you. As Erasmus once said: "A good way to learn something is to study it; even better is to observe it practiced; but best of all is to teach it." Augustine said that giving makes us capable of receiving, and teaching makes us receptive to learning.

The story goes that Alexander the Great dearly loved a beautiful woman named Campaspe. He asked the famous artist, Apelles, to paint her portrait. So, day after day, Apelles studied Campaspe, coming to know her inside and out. And each day as he painted her features on the canvas, her real self was being painted on his heart. He grew deeply in love with her. Alexander became aware of Apelles's love. Feeling sorry for Apelles, not wanting him to be separated from what he had come to care for so deeply, Alexander gave Campaspe to Apelles in marriage. (This is one reason we call him Alexander "the Great.")

I believe, my reader, my friend, that God wants me to paint a beautiful portrait of devotion. This is a subject dear to Him. And I am eager to paint this portrait—yes, to obey God and do my duty, but also because while I am painting spiritual love for others I may hopefully fall in love with it myself. And if God our King sees me fallen deeply in love with spiritual devotion, He will give that quality to me in eternal matrimony.

The chaste and lovely Rebecca, after watering Isaac's camels, was chosen to be his bride, and as a token she received golden earrings and golden bracelets (Gen. 24:22). I desire God to make my soul His bride. I long for Him to place in my ears His words of gold, and to put on my arms the golden power to put His words into action. That power is the seal of true devotion, and I wish it devoutly for myself and all of you.

by Francis de Sales
(Abridged and contemporized by Marvin D. Hinten)

# Chapter 1
*What is Devotion?*

You are interested in the devotional life because you know how much devotion pleases God. Now, one's devotional life is like anything else; if you start out in the wrong direction, even by a little bit, you get continually further off target. There is true devotion, and there is false; unless you learn early to tell the difference, you will spend a great deal of time in wandering (and, even worse, you will not know it).

A certain Roman portrait painter supposedly used to make every portrait resemble the woman he loved; and similarly every person imagines devotion according to his preferences. A person who believes strongly in fasting will consider himself devout if he has fasted, though his heart may be full of spite. Another person may be a temperance fanatic who would not even touch his tongue to wine; but he would get drunk on his neighbor's blood in gossip. Another thinks herself devout because she says so many fervent prayers every day; but when the prayers are over she uses her speech in browbeating employees. Someone else willingly draws money from his account to help the poor; but he can't draw sweetness from his heart to forgive an enemy. Still another is able to pardon enemies, but she doesn't get her bills paid until threatened with a lawsuit.

Often these people make a good appearance of holiness, as when Saul's messengers searched for David in his house. Michal, protecting David, put a dummy in the bed and covered it with blankets, making the messengers believe David was sick (1 Sam. 19:11–14). Similarly, many people cover themselves with outward actions that have an appearance of holiness, and observers believe them to be truly spiritual; but they are really only images of holiness.

True devotion is based on faith in God. In fact, devotion is basically faith extended. Faith makes us acceptable to God through His grace. Devotion is faith developed; a devout person is one advanced in faith. Faith makes us want to serve God; devotion is the state at which we want to serve God repeatedly, promptly, and carefully.

Ostriches don't fly. Chickens can fly, but they prefer not to, and they always do it clumsily. Eagles, however, soar swiftly and constantly. In the same way, unbelievers do not fly to God; they keep an earthly course and direct their attention only to the earth. Believers who are not yet devout attempt to fly to God by their good deeds, but these are brief, low trips. Devout people, however, spend much of their time and energy soaring in the heavens.

Devotion could be termed spiritual adrenaline. Faith makes us want to follow God's ways; devotion makes following God's ways thrilling. Faith makes us willing to keep the commandments; devotion makes us eager to keep the commandments. A person is a believer only if she obeys God; a person is devout only if she gets excited about obeying God. A devout person doesn't just attempt to "keep the commandments"; she does good works promptly and wholeheartedly—not just those she has been told to do, but even the ones that just pop into her head.

A man recovering from a major illness walks because he knows he has to, to recover; but walking is slow and painful for him. A believer recovering from sin obeys because his Physician orders it; but obeying is slow and painful. As the believer (or patient) recovers, however, he begins to run and leap in the commandments. That is devotion.

# Chapter 2
## *Devotion's Excellence*

Ten spies tried to discourage Israel from entering the Promised Land by saying it was a land that "ate up the inhabitants"; in other words, it had giants who would consume them. But Joshua and Caleb declared that not only was the Promised Land good, but it would also be sweet and pleasant to live in.

Similarly, the world defames religious devotion as much as it can, picturing devout people with sour looks, saying that religion is "too depressing." But, according to the Holy Spirit, a devout life is not just good but delightful as well.

The world sees that devout people fast, pray, accept injuries, tend the sick, give to the poor, restrain their passions, hold their tempers, moderate their pleasures, and altogether act in an apparently stifling and unpleasant manner. What the world can't see is an inward devotion that sweetens these acts.

Look at bees on clover. Clover juice is bitter—but the bees work it into honey, because that's their nature. Yes, unbelievers—Christians do find self-denial to be bitter, but they convert it inside (the devout ones do) into sweetness and comfort. Flames and swords seem like blessings to devout martyrs. If death itself can be made sweet by love, what will devotion do to a virtuous action?

As sugar sweetens unripe fruit, devotion is the spiritual sugar that takes the bitterness out of loneliness and oppression. Love is the sweetest of all spiritual sweets. If faith is milk, love is the cream; if faith is a plant, love is the flower; if faith is a gem, love is the radiance.

And loving devotion is fit for any vocation. At the creation God commanded plants to yield after their kind; and so Christians, the plants of His church, will yield fruit after their kind. A factory worker's love for God will be expressed differently from a secretary's, from a homemaker's, from a politician's. Each person's devotion must be adapted to his circumstances. A retailer with a family can't expect to live like a monk, can he? And the factory worker can't spend every day in a church the way the pastor does.

Properly expressed, love doesn't spoil things; it perfects them. When a bee draws its nectar from a flower, the flower isn't hurt. Heavenly love is even better, for it not only doesn't hurt our lives; it improves them. A jewel tossed into honey comes out glistening; and a worker who falls in love with Christ tends to shine. Families become more peaceful, marriages more committed, and employees more faithful in service.

It is wrong to believe that love for Christ can only be expressed in church. Joseph was devout as a carpenter, Lydia as a retailer, and Cornelius as a soldier. We need never excuse ourselves from a devout life because we have jobs.

# Chapter 3
*Cleansing the Soul*

Before a foreign maiden was allowed to marry an Israelite, she had to shave her head, trim her nails, and take off the clothing that captives wore (Deut. 21:12–13). Similarly, a soul that wishes to become the bride of the Son of God must put off the old person and put on the new (Col. 3:9–10). Some people may experience a total overnight change in their thought and behavior; but this is as rare as a resurrection, and most of us can't expect it. Usually healing, whether of body or soul, takes time.

As the sun begins to dawn, it does not switch the landscape from night to day in a flash, but does so little by little. You may recall a proverb we have: "The slow cure is the most sure." Physical, emotional, and spiritual pain are all alike; they charge in on horseback, but they leave on foot.

A person who wants a clean soul needs to be courageous and patient. It makes me so sad to see people become discouraged when they find they still have imperfections after trying for months and years to be devout. They get anxious and downhearted and are tempted to just give up trying.

But, on the other hand, I feel even sadder for those

people who don't recognize their imperfections! They think they are already devout, and try to fly before their wings are fledged. Like people who discontinue a necessary prescription because "I feel fine," they are in danger.

The practice of becoming holy ends only with our lives. Let us not become discouraged by imperfections. Don't you see? Our perfecting process consists of fighting those imperfections. And how can we fight them if we don't find them? And how can we conquer them if we don't meet with them? Our victory consists not in obliviousness to imperfections, but in our desire not to consent to them.

And the battle involves more than just fighting imperfections; sometimes we will be wounded by them. (This keeps us humble.) Yet to be wounded is not to lose the battle. We only lose the battle by being killed or surrendering. Sin wounds but does not kill us spiritually; only leaving Christ can do that.

So, since we can't be killed by sins, the only thing we need to do to win the battle is not to give up. Who could get discouraged in a war like this, when, if we only keep fighting, we can't help but win?

One of our great difficulties in being purified is that we stop sinning, but we wish we still *could* sin. It's like the Israelites, who all left Egypt, but they kept an affection for what Egypt had to offer. That is why even after escaping Egypt they complained in the desert; they fondly thought about the fish, watermelons, onions, and cucumbers that they used to enjoy when they were slaves. And there are people who decide not to sin, but still wistfully think about it. The body withdraws from sin, but the heart keeps stealing backward glances at it, just as Lot's wife had to take a final glimpse of Sodom (Gen. 19:26).

Many of us abstain from sin in the same way that many diabetics abstain from sugar. Diabetics don't eat sugar because the doctor says it will hurt their health. But some diabetics frequently think about sweets, they wish they could have some, they keep wanting to try a little bit of this or that to see if it's as good as it looks; they wonder if they could get away with a small amount "just this once." They consider really lucky the people who can eat sweets without guilt.

That's the way a lot of us abstain from sin. We wish God's laws were a little more lenient. We think people are lucky who can do what we want to but aren't allowed to. We don't take revenge on a person who's been unjust with us. But afterwards we discuss the situation with our friends and say, "Man, if I weren't a Christian, what I would do to him! If I weren't required to forgive him, I sure wouldn't!"

Oh, this poor Christian. He doesn't realize that affection for sin can rob his happiness just as sin itself can. He is out of Egypt, but not happy, because his appetite is still Egyptian, wanting fish and onions. He is like a woman who doesn't intend to have sex, but likes flirting and having men caress her. That's dangerous!

Being purified means not only cleansing your soul of sin, but clearing away the affection for sin. A soul that doesn't sin, but wishes it could, loses Christian joy. It is like run-down, anemic people who eat without enjoying the taste, sleep without gaining rest, and walk without feeling energy.

As we turn on more lights in a room, we can see our faces in a mirror more clearly. And as the Holy Spirit enlightens our consciences, we can see more clearly our spiritual blemishes. And as we see ourselves more clearly, we must get rid of not only our sins but our pleasure in getting away with sin. It is not only wrong to lie; it is wrong to be afterwards relieved that our lie got us out of a tight spot. We all know it is wrong for a person to enjoy displeasing God. So isn't it wrong for a person to enjoy a comfort that comes from displeasing God?

"Dead flies give perfume a bad smell," the Bible notes (Eccles. 10:1 NIV); in other words, flies buzzing over or even landing near the perfume are not the problem, but those that get trapped in it. One can compare this to bad thoughts. We all have inappropriate thoughts come into our minds from time to time. While these, like flies, are a nuisance, they are not the real spiritual danger. That comes from the thoughts that get stuck in our minds. Our goal should be to build spiritual spiderwebs through a desire for mental purity; when the flies hit these webs, they will not then land permanently in our minds, rotting away.

Games, feasts, comedies, and other forms of entertainment are not in themselves bad things; they can be used well or badly. But to be too fond of them is dangerous. It is not evil to engage in entertainment, but it is evil to overcommit one's heart to it.

Stags that have put on too much fall fat retire to the thickets, knowing that they would not be in fit shape to run if they were attacked. And a person's heart, if she has it weighted down with superfluous affections, is not eager and ready to run after God. Little children amuse themselves by running after lightning bugs; no one finds fault with it, because they are children. But if grownups spent most of their time chasing after lightning bugs, wouldn't that look ridiculous? Entertainment does not conflict with spiritual love, but devotion to entertainment does.

# Chapter 4
## *Prayer*

Our minds are spiritually ignorant; our wills are corrupt. But prayer places our understanding in the brightness of divine light and warms our will with heavenly love. Prayer is the rain of God. It sprinkles on our good desires so that they bud and blossom, and it washes our souls of impurities.

The kind of prayer I recommend more than any other is meditating on the life and death of Jesus. By gazing on Him frequently, you will learn His ways, form your actions on His model, and fill your whole mind with Him. He is the Light of the world; it is through Him that we should seek to be enlightened.

Children, by listening to their parents and making similar noises, learn to speak the language. We, living near the Lord in meditation, observing His words, actions, and affections, will learn by His grace to like, do, and speak the things that He does.

Begin all kinds of prayer by invoking God's presence. Don't try to fit in a whole "prayer list," but think through what you are saying. A single paragraph well-considered is better than several recited quickly.

If you don't have a chance to pray in the morning,

then make time in the evening. But don't try to pray right after a heavy meal: You'll get too sleepy.

You may not even know how to pray privately; for I'm afraid few people in our time do. So I will present you with some simple helps for starting. (There are some excellent books written on prayer that will help you further, and, of course, practice perfects.)

How does one prepare for prayer? You do two things. First, you place yourself in God's presence; and second, you ask for His help in preparing.

Placing yourself in God's presence means recognizing, first of all, that God is everywhere. God is present wherever we are just as air is present wherever birds fly. We all know this truth, but we don't always grasp it. Blind people cannot see a king enter a room, though naturally they will pay their respects when told of his presence. But because they do not see him, they can easily forget he is present, and as they forget they will tend to behave as though he were not there.

Alas! God is present with us, but we do not see Him. Faith informs us He is here; but since we can't see Him with our eyes, we often forget Him and behave as though God were not around. We know, intellectually, that God is everywhere. But when we are not thinking about it, it is as if we didn't know it. For this reason, we must start our prayers by remembering that God has all day been with us. We can use the words of Jacob: "Surely the LORD is in this place, and I was not aware of it. . . . How awesome is this place!" (Gen. 28:16–17 NIV).

With the knowledge of God's presence, you then reverently ask His help in praying, recognizing your unworthiness to be in the presence of such great majesty. Yet this majesty wills you to be in His presence. Knowing this, you can ask for help in adoring and serving Him. You can use the words of David: "Give me understanding, and I will keep your law and obey it with all my heart" (Ps. 119:34 NIV).

After invoking God's presence, it is good to begin your prayers with meditation, which means thinking on the things of God in order to increase our affection for Him. Thus does meditation differ from study, which is generally done to become knowledgeable, or to teach a class, or to write. Admittedly, some things regarding God are awfully hard to meditate on: His greatness, the beauty of His virtue, and the love that led Him to create us, to give three examples. I don't want meditation to appear intellectually impossible! In cases like these, use an analogy; use what you know about in life to capture a glimpse of what God may be like. Think about a powerful person, for instance, and then consider how much more powerful is God. If you find an analogy particularly useful in helping you appreciate God, don't rush away from it to "get in your prayers"; reflect on it for a while.

Meditation is geared toward our will. It builds up in us love for God or a neighbor, desire for heaven, zeal for salvation of souls, compassion, joy, a desire to imitate Christ's life, remorse for our past evil ways, hatred of sin, fear of God's judgment, and trust in His goodness and mercy. Meditation ought to expand, to open up our spiritual affections.

But you must not simply dwell in these general affections without converting them into specific resolutions for change. For instance, you may meditate on our Lord's first saying on the cross: "Father, forgive them, for they do not know what they are doing" (Luke 23:34 NIV). This will doubtless cause you to want to imitate Christ. You will desire to forgive your enemies and love them as much as He did.

That desire is not worth much unless you then make a specific application. You may say, "All right. From now on, when my employees complain about my ways of doing things, I will not take offense. When such-and-such a person makes me feel small, I will not grow incensed. On the contrary, I will plan to do this or that thing that may serve to soften him." And you plan specific responses to other trials. Using this means, you can achieve spiritual growth in a short time, whereas with mere vague desires growth comes slowly and with difficulty.

When you conclude your prayers, thank God for the thoughts He has given you. Praise Him for the goodness and mercy you have recognized. Offer up to Him the spiritual desires and resolutions you have formed, supporting them by appealing to God's mercy, Christ's virtue, and His purifying death. Ask God to place within you the graces of His Son and to bless your resolutions so that you may be able to perform them. Pray these things for the church as well, for pastors, relatives, and friends.

Finally, as you finish praying, gather what I call a bouquet of devotion. Here's what I mean. People who have a beautiful flower garden do not like to leave it outside while they must be inside. So they gather some flowers to bring inside, to smell and enjoy as they go about their work. In the same way, when we have finished praying, we ought to pick out one or two points that have been most meaningful to us, to take with us the rest of the day. If we fix these particular thoughts in our minds, we will be able to continue enjoying them after our prayer time is over.

When you have finished praying, keep in mind the resolutions you have made. If you make resolutions in prayer without attempting to carry them out, you will believe yourself to be better than you are, for most of us think we *really* are what we have decided we want to be. Thus it is necessary to seek opportunities to put our resolutions into practice, even in small ways. For example, if I have decided to respond gently to someone who offends me, I shall try to meet him during the day so I can greet him in a friendly manner. And if I cannot meet him personally, I shall at least try to say something nice about him to someone.

Try to learn to pass smoothly back and forth between prayer and work. Job requirements usually seem to us a great deal removed from personal devotions. But a lawyer should know how to switch from prayer to debating, a retail worker from prayer to ringing up a sale, a homemaker from prayer to vacuuming, and all of them back again, smoothly and peacefully. Work and prayer are both done within God's will.

# Chapter 5
## *Further Thoughts on Prayer*

In addition to your complete and formal prayer time, you should pray briefly at other opportunities throughout the day. These are like shoots that spring out of your main prayer root.

In the morning, it is good to prepare for the day. Thank God for preserving you through the night, and if you recall any sin from the previous evening, ask His pardon.

Recognize that the present day has been given as a sort of down payment on eternity and determine to employ it as such. Think over the day's business, the opportunities you will have to serve God, and the temptations to offend Him. Determine to use the opportunities to become more devoted; resolve to avoid, resist, or conquer the temptations.

Again, do not just make a resolution, but think about means of putting it into practice. For instance, if I will be dealing during the day with someone who has a hot temper, I will not just resolve to maintain self-control. I will prepare calming words in anticipation, or I will try to have someone else around who can smooth out the situation. If there is someone sick that I need to visit, I will decide what time to go, and what I might bring, and plan something reassuring to say.

Having done this, you then paradoxically humble yourself before God and admit that you can't follow through on what you've just decided to do, either to resist evil or to do good. As if you were holding up your heart in your hands, offer all your good intentions to the divine majesty. Ask Him to protect and strengthen them so that you may succeed in serving Him.

In the evening, thank God for His preservation during the day. Examine your behavior, which you can do more easily if you recall what you did during the day and with whom.

If you find you have done something good during the day, thank God for it. If you have done some evil, confess it and determine to correct it at the first opportunity.

During the day, let your thoughts ascend briefly but frequently to God. Ask His help, be impressed with Him, remember the cross, adore His goodness, anticipate salvation with Him, stretch out your hand to let Him lead you as a father does a little child. When we spend time with God regularly, we take on the "scent" of His perfections. These quick ascensions can be interspersed throughout our work without interfering with it. In fact, an appropriate pause can further our efforts. A distance runner who takes a sip of water to refresh his mouth is not interrupting his running but receiving strength for it. I am not suggesting an extended thought toward God but a sentence of praise, a quick apology, a passing greeting.

A woman in love is always thinking about her boyfriend or fiancé, always feeling affectionate toward him. She talks about him frequently and writes his name over and over in her journal. Similarly, those who love God are always thinking about Him, always wanting Him around, and wishing they could write His name on the hearts of everyone they know.

God is moved by our words to the extent that we are moved by His. Be attentive, then, to God's words, whether you hear them in a sermon or in conversation. Use those words to your profit. Do not let them fall to the ground, but apply them like salve to your soul. Treasure these matters in your heart, as Jesus' mother Mary did.

And always have near you some good book of devotion. Read it as if it were a letter sent from heaven to encourage you to walk in the heavenly way. Read histories and biographies of devout Christians, which is like watching a drama on how to live the Christian life. Try to work their actions into your particular circumstances. Naturally, some lives you will learn more from than others, but in virtually any devout saint you will observe one key characteristic—a powerful pervasive desire to be loved by God.

Three actions take place when a woman becomes engaged: She hears the proposal, she decides whether she likes the idea, and she consents. The same three steps are involved in sin: We are tempted, we decide whether we want to follow the temptation, and we do it. And the same three steps take place when God wishes us to be devout: He inspires us to love Him, we decide whether we want to love, and we do it.

Inspiration to love should last our whole lives, and a person who enjoys being inspired pleases God. God would be offended, on the other hand, with a long-term steady who didn't want to actually marry Him. That was why God became offended with the Israelites; He had tried to "pop the question" for years, and they wouldn't even listen. A man who has dated a woman for years would be understandably hurt if he told her he'd like to discuss marriage, and she said she wasn't interested.

Delighting in thoughts that draw us to God is a great

first step toward pleasing Him. Obviously, attraction to obedience is not the same as obeying. Yet the attraction certainly makes obedience more likely. So when an impulse to do something loving enters your heart, listen to it. Entertain it as an ambassador from a great king, with an offer of marriage. And accept it.

Sometimes your spirit will seem "dry"; you will not enjoy prayer, and it will not mean anything to you. Don't become distressed. Just pray out loud, telling God your disappointment, confessing your unworthiness to receive, yet asking His help.

Sometimes, reading a Christian book will help. Read it attentively until you come to a part that moves your spirit. Sometimes a gesture or movement will help—lying face down before the Lord, for instance.

If, after all this, you still don't seem to get anything out of prayer—then don't worry about it. Just continue to come into God's presence with reverence. Think how many courtiers there are who go a hundred times a year to visit the king, not expecting to be permitted to speak with him, but only wanting to pay their respects and let him know they're still around! So ought we to be willing to come to prayer, simply to pay our respects and bear witness to our faithfulness. If it should please the divine majesty to speak to us, that is a great honor and pleasure. But if He does not choose to give us this grace, and He seems to ignore us, we still ought not to leave. On the contrary, we ought simply to rest in His presence, devout and peaceful. Infallibly, He will note our perseverance. At another time, when we return, He will console us and entice us with sweetness. But when He does not do so, let us remind ourselves that it is a great honor simply to be near Him.

## Chapter 6
*Confession and Communion*

The sins you confess may be small. But no matter how small they are, dislike them intensely. Don't just confess sins, but think about ways to correct them. Otherwise you'll spend your whole life doing the same sins over and over. The reason for confessing a sin is to be cleansed of it—not just of that particular instance, but of the sin itself.

Do not just make vague accusations against yourself the way a lot of Christians do. "I ought to love God more than I do." "I'm sorry I don't pray like I should." "I need to be a better Christian." Making confessions such as these is a means of avoiding confession; the purest saint who ever lived could accuse herself in vague generalities like these! Turn, instead, to some specific fault; when you have discovered it, then confess it frankly.

For example, let us suppose you accuse yourself of not loving your friends the way you should. Perhaps your conscience is bothering you because a friend mentioned a medical bill he couldn't get paid, and though you had the means, you didn't offer to help. Instead of speaking in general terms, accuse yourself of this specifically. Say, "This friend told me he couldn't pay his bill. But I didn't offer to help because I've been saving up money for a new VCR" (or because he isn't that close a friend, or whatever the reason is). Similarly, do not confess a "poor prayer life"; if you're allowing something in the room to distract you, or if you have not allowed sufficient time, or if you have not made the effort to plan your prayer times, then confess that.

And do not simply state the fact of your sins, but explore the reasons behind them. For example, do not say only that you lied, but determine whether you lied to keep yourself out of trouble, or to make a story sound better, or to make yourself look impressive. If you cheated during a game, determine whether it was because you're too attached to winning, or you were mad at the opponent's taunts, or you just wanted to see if you could get away with it; and so on.

Be honest. If a man who gets on my nerves makes a joke about something I did, I tend to grow angry and try to get him back for it, excusing myself because he started it. But then I realize that if a favorite friend of mine said the same thing, I would let it pass. Thus I confess, "I have gotten mad at this man, not because of what he said, but because I dislike him as a person." Attempt to discover not only sins, but roots of sins.

About communion. It is told of Mithridates, king of Pontus many centuries ago, that he took a little bit of poison each day to protect himself from assassination. Eventually his body grew used to it. Finally, according to the story, when the Romans took over Pontus and planned to make Mithridates their slave, he tried to poison himself for real. But he couldn't do it; his body had become too strong.

Our Savior has instituted a sacrament of communion with His body and blood, so that the person who eats and drinks it will be similarly immune to death. A person who takes communion frequently strengthens the health of her soul, becoming ever more immune to the poison of evil affections.

Apricots and strawberries are tender and prone to decay. But they may be easily kept all year when preserved in sugar. It is not surprising, then, that our hearts, which are also prone to corruption, can be kept preserved from the rottenness of sin by the sweetness of communion with Christ.

On days when you will be receiving communion, prepare for it before the event. Confess your sins, and as you partake, remember Christ. By participating in this beautiful sacrament often, you will yourself turn beautiful.

# Chapter 7
*Virtue*


When love enters our hearts it is always accompanied by a host of other virtues. And it begins putting them to work, as a captain does his soldiers. But it does not put all the virtues to work all the time. The righteous is "like a tree planted by streams of water, which yields its fruit in season" (Ps. 1:3 NIV). And love, in a person's soul, brings forth virtuous works that are in season.

As the old proverb goes, "Music is pleasant, but not to a person in mourning." It is a great fault in some Christians that whenever they have learned to practice a spiritual virtue, they want to put it into practice on every occasion. They're like the ancient philosophers who attempted to maintain a stoic face on every occasion. Worse yet, these Christians criticize others who aren't exercising the same virtues they are. But we should "rejoice with those who rejoice; mourn with those who mourn" (Rom. 12:15 NIV). "Love does not insist on its own way" (1 Cor. 13:5).

There are, however, virtues that do have an almost universal application. We do not find many opportunities to practice courage or generosity; but honesty, humility, gentleness, and temperance ought to color our entire lives. There may be more impressive virtues; but these are the ones we need every day. Sugar tastes better than salt; but salt is used more in everyday foods.

We should try to exercise virtues that are necessary to our circumstances and not just the ones to our taste. The apostles were commissioned to preach the gospel. They were right in asserting that they should not take time away from this to care for the poor, no matter how important caring for the poor might be (Acts 6:2). Every profession needs the virtues in varying degrees; a pastor exercises them in one way, a widow in another, and a soldier in a third. Although all ought to strive for every Christian virtue, all ought not to attempt to practice them equally, but each should concentrate on the virtues fit for her particular calling.

Among Christian virtues, we should prefer the most excellent ones and not the most showy. Comets usually appear larger than the stars, but they are really not larger, just more spectacular. Most people are more impressed by virtue that can be seen—fasting, giving money, church attendance, acts of overt self-denial. Less appreciated but more excellent are the inner virtues—modesty, kindliness, and spiritual self-denial. People serve God in a variety of ways: by serving the sick, relieving the poor, teaching Christianity to children, recovering the lost, maintaining church buildings, promoting peace. They are all like embroiderers weaving lovely patterns on a variety of backgrounds.

Augustine says that people who eventually wind up as devout Christians tend to start by going too far. It's true; people recently come out of sin into committed Christianity tend to have excessive scruples. This is a tendency I prefer in young Christians, provided they lose it as they mature. In a Christian heart, little by little, love should drive out servile fear.

Bernard, in his early days as head of a monastery, was quite severe with those under his guidance. Right from the start he told them they ought to leave behind their bodies and come to him solely as spirits. When they confessed sins to him, he despised every fault, no matter how small. Bernard so severely chastised his people and so sharply urged them to perfection that he actually drove them away from it. They lost heart when they saw how steep an ascent was being placed before them. Zeal led Bernard to urge his people on, and ordinarily zeal is a virtue, but in this case it needed to be rebuked.

Eventually God Himself corrected Bernard of it. He gave to Bernard a sweet, gracious, tender spirit, that caused an obvious change in this man. Bernard began accusing himself of having been too stern. He was, after this, so gracious and gentle with everyone that it was said he, like Paul, became all things to gain all men.

Jerome wrote an epitaph for the saintly Paula in which he tells us that she went too far in the practice of some virtues. She buffeted her body until her pastor had to ask her to stop, and even then she wouldn't. She was brokenhearted over the death of friends who died without Christ, so much so that whenever a friend died, Paula was in danger of death herself.

Jerome concludes his epitaph this way: "It will be said that instead of writing the praises of this saint, I am writing accusations and reproaches. I call as witness Jesus, whom she served and whom I desire to serve, that I am not trying to light on either the side of praise or blame. I say simply what a Christian man observed in a Christian woman. That is to say, I write history, not eulogy. And what are vices in her would have been virtues in others."

He means that what was a fault in Paula would have been a virtue in a person less spiritually advanced. There certainly are actions praiseworthy in beginning Christians that would be imperfections in a person more mature. When a person who has just swallowed poison induces vomiting, we approve of his action. But if the person has recently swallowed nothing harmful, and yet continues to induce vomiting, we worry about him. We should always think well of others who are attempting to practice virtues, even if they're going too far, for every great saint began this way. But for ourselves, we should attempt to practice virtues not just faithfully but wisely. To assure this, we should lean not on our own understanding, but consult the wisdom of mature Christian friends.

I want to say a word about some things that many Christians regard as being virtues, but they really aren't. I am referring to trances, visions, ecstatic tongues-speaking, and other raptures of a similar nature. These ecstasies are not virtues, though they might be considered rewards God gives to virtue. Actually, it would be better to consider them samples of future happiness which are sometimes shown to men to increase their desire for the totality of rapture in heaven.

Anyway, we ought not to try to work at getting such gifts, since they're not really necessary to serve and love God (which ought to be our only goal). Rapturous gifts can't really be gained by working at them, since they are something we receive, rather than working out in ourselves. When it comes to work, all we can do is work at being devout. If God chooses to give us angelic gifts—why, then we shall try to be devout angels. But in the meantime, let us try to develop purity, chastity, diligence, zeal, and tolerance of our neighbors' imperfections.

Let us willingly leave the lofty celestial peaks to those whom God chooses to exalt there. We don't "deserve" any special rank in the kingdom of God. Let us be happy to be His "gophers," to wash dishes in His kitchen, to deliver His packages. It is up to Him, if He thinks it good, to select us into His cabinet.

God cares less about the dignity of people's positions

than about the love and humility with which they carry their positions out. How did Rebecca become Abraham's daughter-in-law? Through volunteering to water his camels. Saul was chosen as the first king of Israel while looking for some missing livestock of his father's. Ruth became Boaz's wife after gathering up leftover grain in a field.

People who believe they are "chosen" for supernatural experiences are subject to delusions. In fact, those who think themselves like angels are sometimes not even good human beings! Their phrases are loftier than their thoughts and deeds. But let us not censure anyone rashly; let us thank God that He elevates some, and let us be content to walk on a path lower but surer. If we walk this path faithfully, God will be the One to raise us.

# Chapter 8
## *Patient Endurance*

"Consider him [Jesus] who endured such opposition from sinful men, so that you will not grow weary and lose heart" (Heb. 12:3 NIV).

"You need to persevere so that when you have done the will of God, you will receive what he has promised" (Heb. 10:36 NIV).

Our Savior saved us through enduring suffering, that we should likewise be able to endure injury and affliction with as much gentleness as possible.

Don't limit your patience only to certain kinds of injuries or afflictions, but patiently accept whatever God sends you or permits to reach you. Some people are only willing to take honorable trials. They would be willing to suffer persecution for their religious beliefs, but not for any other reason. A true suffering servant of God bears equally with honorable and embarrassing trials. Any decent Christian can shrug off being reproved and accused by the wicked. But to patiently endure reproof and accusation from good people, from friends, from relatives—this is where Christianity comes in.

I remember a preacher some years ago named Carl Borromeo. He was attacked by a good many people, and he took all the attacks meekly. But I most respect his patience when he was publicly attacked by another preacher in his denomination over a theological dispute. Bees are greater insects than gnats, so their stings are sharper. And the wrongs we receive from good people are far harder to bear than wrongs from others. Sometimes it happens that two basically good people, with excellent intentions, create persecution and opposition for each other because of differing opinions.

Be patient not only regarding what happens to you, but also regarding circumstances that arise from the initial affliction. Many people are willing to bear some inconvenience from evil, but not "the last straw."

"I wouldn't mind being poor," one says, "if it weren't for wanting my kids to grow up in a nicer neighborhood."

Another says, "I wouldn't mind losing my job if only people knew it wasn't my fault."

And another asserts, "I don't mind her saying such terrible things about me; I'm just afraid somebody will believe them."

"I don't mind being sick," says one more, "but I hate being a burden to my family."

I say, if we are going to endure with Christian patience, we must uncomplainingly accept not only being ill, but the illness God wishes, and the time He wishes, and around the people He wishes, and with the inconveniences He wishes. And so on with every other form of trouble.

When affliction comes to you, feel free to resist it with remedies that are available and within God's will. But then await with complete resignation the result God allows. If the remedies win, thank Him humbly. If the affliction wins, bless Him patiently.

Regarding accusation, I follow Gregory's advice. If you are accused of a fault justly, then humble yourself and admit that you have done it. If you are accused falsely, then gently deny it, for this is a duty you owe to truth and to your neighbor's knowledge. If, after your true denial, you are still accused, do not trouble yourself about it at all, and don't try to press home your denial. Having done your duty to the truth, you now must do your duty to humility. If you follow this advice, you will have done the proper things to protect both your reputation and your sense of peace.

Complain as little as possible about wrong that has been done to you. As a rule, whoever complains commits sin, for self-love always makes injuries sting more deeply than they really should. If you feel you must complain, either to come to terms with the situation or to set the wrong aright, complain to someone who is calm and loves God. Never complain to a person who is ready to be indignant and think evil. Instead of soothing your wound, they will make you feel it more painfully. Instead of removing the thorn that pricks you, they'll just push it deeper into your foot.

Many people, when they are sick or have experienced injustice, do not complain—but they still find ways to make people feel sorry for them. If they're going to be patient, they want other people to notice how patient they're being. This "patience" is actually nothing more than vanity. A truly patient sufferer speaks of her condition without complaining or exaggerating. If anyone feels sorry for her, she accepts it, unless they're feeling sorry for something that isn't really hurting her, and then she gently notes that she isn't suffering in that way. A patient sufferer is at peace with the truth.

In the sufferings that come to you as a devout person (and there will be sufferings), remember the word of God: "A woman giving birth to a child has pain because her time has come; but when her baby is born she forgets the anguish because of her joy that a child is born into the world" (John 16:21 NIV). Your soul has conceived the most worthy child in the world—Jesus Christ. He will be born when He entirely rules your heart, and your life is an imitation of His. But before this blessed event, you are going to have labor pains. Be courageous; for when the pains have passed, eternal joy will rest on you for having given birth to such a child in such a world.

# Chapter 9
*Humility*

When a poor widow asked Elisha how to get help, he said, "Go around and ask all your neighbors for empty jars. Don't ask for just a few" (2 Kings 4:3 NIV). To receive God's grace our hearts must be empty of pride.

The greatest saints have always honored humility above the other moral virtues. Some people are proud of always being well-dressed or of having a nice car; why can't they see how silly this is? If anyone deserves credit in a case like this, it would be the dress or the car. It's incredible, how we humans tend to borrow our value from a piece of metal or cloth!

Pride is like an ice cube; when dropped into water, the cube bobs around the surface of the water and stays visible. If you want to know whether you are humble, examine your generosity and knowledge to see whether they are always noticeable, continually bobbing around the surface.

If we try to get other people to notice us, we lose the glory of our virtues. Honor is beautiful when offered freely, and ugly when extracted from others like a tooth. A flower in the earth gives a pleasing fragrance; but if it could convince all passersby to pluck it up, handle it, and examine it, soon it would wither away.

The pursuit of virtue makes us holy; the pursuit of attention makes us contemptible. A person who is collecting pearls doesn't bother loading himself down with shells; and a person who is after holiness doesn't load himself down with other people's notice. Those who desire virtue don't refuse honor when it comes; they just don't go out of their way looking for it.

On the other hand, a lot of people try not to think about the different gifts and abilities God has provided them with, to avoid pride. This is a mistake. We are drawn to love God through considering His benefits; thus, as Aquinas observed, the more we recognize what God has done for us, the more we will love Him. Since the blessings He has given us will move us more emotionally than what He's done for others, we ought to reflect most on what He's done for us. If we want to be humble before God's justice, we will consider the multitude of our sins; if we want to be humble before God's grace, we will consider the multitude of our blessings.

If we are going to think about what we've done against Him, we need also to think about what He's done for us. If we go over our sins specifically, we ought also to go over His favors specifically. We don't need to fear that a recognition of our talents will make us proud, as long as we see that the good in us does not come from ourselves. You can perfume a mule, but everyone still knows it's a mule.

Often we confess that in ourselves we are nothing, the trash of the world, spiritually speaking; but we would feel hurt if anyone really believed it of us. We cut ourselves down so that the world can pick us back up. We should get used to saying words only if we genuinely mean them and want them to be believed.

Perhaps at this point I should add that sometimes we use words without much meaning for the sake of simple courtesy. When you start a letter with "Dear," that doesn't necessarily mean the person is dear to you; it's a way of showing respect. It's perfectly all right to use words and phrases that are slightly exaggerated when people recognize those words simply as a custom. In general, however, our words should match our sentiments as closely as possible.

Another scruple which sometimes causes people trouble is this: What if we think someone could be helped by knowing something we've done, but it's something that makes us look good? Should a teacher, for instance, in a lesson on courage, mention a time she has been courageous if she thinks it will be helpful as an example for others?

Certainly. Humility means that we hide our virtues most of the time, even when we want to flaunt them, but we bring them out when that will serve God's kingdom, even if talking about ourselves that way makes us uncomfortable. Does it seem foolish to you that sometimes we Christians hide our virtues and other times we bring out into the open what we've kept hidden for years? Don't let feeling foolish stop you from doing what's right! If you're acting with a sincere heart before God, then do what you believe will support His work, even if to an unbeliever you seem inconsistent.

Someone nominated for a church office or asked to serve in some way may say, "I just don't think I'm good enough to do that." Sometimes this is a false humility to disguise the fact that they simply don't want to do it, or are too lazy to take the task on, or perhaps simply don't care enough about God to want to serve Him. A good Biblical example of this is Ahaz. Isaiah said to encourage his faith, "Ask the LORD your God for a sign." Ahaz answered, "I will not ask; I will not put the LORD to the test." This sounds like great reverence and humility, but Isaiah recognized this was just Ahaz's way of escaping what God wanted him to do, saying, "Will you try the patience of my God?" (Isa. 7:11–13 NIV).

God desires us to be perfect. A person who thinks of

himself as a good man says perfection is too lofty a goal; he's content just to be a decent Christian. Actually, he's afraid that if he really tries to be perfect, and thinks about what that means, he'll find weaknesses in himself that he never noticed before! But a humble man, who thinks of himself as morally wretched, doesn't mind taking a shot at perfection. What does he have to lose? And in some area of weakness, God may just jump in and surprise him.

Some of the evils we put up with in this world are respectable; others are embarrassing. Our task is to cheerfully put up with both. Not having a job, for instance, is financially painful; having people think you don't have a job because you're not trying hard enough to get one is emotionally painful. A sore on your thigh causes physical pain; a sore on your face adds emotional pain, because you feel awkward about your appearance. Patience learns to be at peace with physical and financial pain, but only humility has peace amidst emotional pain. If you fall down clumsily in front of a group of people, your emotional discomfort will probably outweigh your physical hurt. Learn to love the embarrassment of it! Do you ever accidentally say something silly or do something stupid? Learn to love it when that happens—what a great opportunity to get humble in a hurry!

You might ask at this point, "But what about my good name? What about my reputation?" A reputation is like hair, a mere adornment—and in Psalm 52:2 David compares a slanderous tongue to a sharpened razor. So what if a person trims away a bit of your hair by teasing you? It'll grow back! The only way your reputation suffers any real damage is if the root of your reputation—that is, yourself —goes bad. When your hair gets torn out by the roots, it doesn't grow back very well. So don't overestimate the importance of reputation—a hundred pounds of it can't measure up to an ounce of humility!

# Chapter 10
*Gentleness*


Just as humility builds our relationship with God, gentleness builds our relationships with others. "Learn from me," Jesus said, "for I am gentle and humble in heart" (Matt. 11:29 NIV). Most Christians think of themselves as gentle, and they really are—unless someone contradicts them or puts them down. Then they swell up like someone bitten by a poisonous snake! Humility and gentleness are the antidotes to poisonous words, keeping us from swelling with anger or irritation.

When Joseph sent his brothers back from Egypt to his father's house, he gave them only one piece of advice: "Don't quarrel on the way!" (Gen 45:24 NIV). I say the same. This life is only a journey to the life that is coming. Let us, as Christian brothers and sisters, not quarrel on the way. Never be angry—never! "Man's anger does not bring about the righteous life that God desires" (James 1:20 NIV). Yes, we must resist evil, but even that with compassion and gentleness. The best object to absorb force is thick wool. When a person criticizes us because he is mad, we don't listen, even if the criticism is deserved, whereas a calm man we would listen to. We want to be treated as reasonable beings, and will at least give audience to the words of reason; but our minds refuse to learn from outbursts. A son will listen and respond to a peaceful father; but if he sees the father come carrying a whip, he will say anything to escape. His only thought is to avoid that whip.

Perhaps there are times when anger seems to be justified. But remember this; anger grows quickly. It is best to make your point without it; for if you allow it in, anger tends to stay. And remember this, too: There has never been an angry man in the history of the world who did not feel his anger was justified. The longer you think about a situation, the more additional reasons you can find to be really mad about it. It's better to find a way to live without anger than to allow it in your mind and attempt to control it.

If you find yourself getting mad about something, what should you do? Ask God to calm the storm inside you. When the disciples found themselves in a storm on the sea, they asked Jesus to help them, and He simply told the tempest to stop, and it did. What Jesus can do for external storms of weather, He can do for internal storms of passion.

One of the most important ways for us to be gentle is toward ourselves. We ought not to continually berate ourselves for our imperfections. Certainly we must be sorry for our sins. Yet many people worry about their inability to overcome worry! They get mad at themselves for not being able to control their tempers! Thus they keep their hearts continually steeped in passion. Why do we become so upset with ourselves? It is self-love; we are disturbed to find that we are imperfect. We must be displeased with our faults, but we must correct them in a rational way—just as a judge does not mete out punishment by how much the act disgusts him, but by what it deserves. We must endeavor most to correct, not those faults that we find personally upsetting, but those that most draw us from Christ. A person on a diet will berate herself vigorously for her lack of self-control over a bowl of ice cream; yet she will gripe about her boss all day without even seeing it as a fault.

Do you want to change your heart? Treat it like a child. Don't yell at it for being so bad; encourage it to get better.

If I had resolved not to cite my accomplishments so much, and yet found myself doing it again, I would not react against myself in this way: "Francis, you vile excuse for a human being, have you been talking about how good you are *again?* You said you weren't going to do that anymore. Liar! Go hide in a hole like the vermin you are."

Instead I would have compassion on myself as I would on anyone else: "Oh, poor Francis, here we've done the very thing we were trying to avoid! Here, I'll help you up, so we can try again. Let's ask God for mercy; He really is going to help us, you know. We *will* get better."

Remember—a heart hurts when it falls. Lift it back up gently; it's tender. Hate falling; hate the way you've hurt God; but don't hate yourself. Instead, encourage yourself, humbly confident in God's mercy, to begin again the path of virtue.

# Chapter 11
*Obedience*

We should care about our spiritual welfare; but we must not confuse caring and worrying. The angels care about our spiritual welfare, but they are not agitated by anxiety. Love and concern are compatible; but joy and anxiety are incompatible. A person can care about someone and still have peace, but a person cannot worry about someone and have peace.

When our Lord reprimanded Martha, He said, "Martha, Martha, you are worried and upset about many things" (Luke 10:41 NIV). She would not have been "upset" if she had merely been concerned. She was overly concerned; she had upset herself and thus received this reprimand from the Lord. Summer showers green up the meadows and make the corn grow; but torrential downpours dig gullies through the fields. Similarly, work done too frantically is not work well done. "It is not good to have zeal without knowledge," Solomon says, "nor to be hasty and miss the way" (Prov. 19:2 NIV). Drones make more noise and flit around more than other bees, and yet all they produce is wax, never honey.

Flies do not bother us because they are strong, but because there are so many of them. Similarly, we are not as troubled by one major concern as by a host of trifling details. Therefore, undertake your affairs with a peaceful mind. Do things one at a time. If you attempt to do everything at once, your spirit will become overcharged.

In everything rely wholly on God. Nevertheless, work quietly on your part as a cooperation with God. He will then give the success that is best for you (though from your point of view it may seem like success or it may seem like failure).

While love is the greatest virtue, obedience can be a useful tool in arriving at it; obedience humbles the heart. It can be either necessary or voluntary.

Necessary obedience refers to the obedience we give to people out of duty, such as bosses, pastors, police officers, and (while we still are living at home) parents. It's necessary obedience in that God has placed these people over us to direct us in their particular sphere. We need to obey their commands; but to really act like Christians, we also ought to ask for and follow their advice, and try to carry out their wishes (to the extent wisdom permits).

For instance, suppose a worship leader in a church service asks us to stand up. We should go along with that, even if standing up is not our preference at the time (unless disability or old age prevents us from readily doing so). If the worship leader wishes us to clap, we should clap. And so on.

The highest obedience, of course, occurs when you obey even though you really don't want to. For a real challenge, try obeying an unpleasant task (1) cheerfully (2) immediately (3) without griping to your superior (4) without griping to anyone else! Do it for the love of Jesus, who for love of us accepted an obedience that led to death on the cross. As Bernard put it, Jesus would rather obey than live.

Voluntary obedience, the other kind I spoke of earlier,

refers to yielding obedience to people that we're not required to—friends, colleagues, and siblings, for instance.
If they want you to do something a bit inconvenient, and
you manage to do it to bring them pleasure, you'll find
the practice makes it easier to follow through on necessary
obedience.

# Chapter 12
## *Chastity*

Chastity is radiant, honorable, beautiful—the lily of virtues! And it's not just for singles; married people can practice chastity as well, although naturally it takes a different form in marriage.

Marriage makes sexual pleasure holy, and husbands and wives should strive to keep it that way. The first step, obviously, is for spouses to avoid seeking sexual pleasure outside their marriages; but even within the marriage bond, spouses should engage in sex in a way that strengthens the relationship rather than causing dissension.

Marital chastity, then, demands not abstinence but self-control—which sometimes can be more challenging than simple abstinence. Marriage indeed provides sexual release and pleasure; but it also involves the complications of determining what times are appropriate, how one's spouse can best be pleased, what honors God, and other matters that require wisdom.

In part, marriage was set up as a sexual release, and, used properly, it serves that purpose well. But the pleasures involved in sex can easily lead people to wonder what pleasures might be found with other partners; and of course, sometimes husbands and wives may be separated because of illness or other circumstances. People who have become used to lovemaking on a regular basis can find the sudden cessation of it difficult.

Catherine of Siena said she believed lots of people lose their relationship with God from first breaking their marriage vows and losing their relationship with their spouse. It's not that adultery is the "ultimate sin," or anything like that—I judge murder and blasphemy to be worse, for instance—but people who sin by adultery often justify it in ways murderers and blasphemers do not. Adulterers find ways to salve their consciences. And whereas murder, say, seems big and is a brief though traumatic episode, adultery seems a relatively minor matter, and therefore people may continue in an affair over a period of time. That repetition confirms their turning away from God's glory.

God says in Matthew that the pure in heart shall see Him; I take this purity to refer primarily to sexual purity.

Sexual temptation is admittedly an attractive one, hard to resist. Human bodies are like water glasses; it's hard to carry glasses together, touching one another, without taking a chance of one of them getting damaged. Or, to use a different analogy, human bodies are like healthy pieces of fruit—good in themselves, but if the pieces of fruit are carelessly allowed to bump into one another with frequency, they become bruised and are lessened in value.

Never allow anyone to touch you improperly, then, at a tender moment of affection. Immodesty takes some of the innocence and freshness away from chastity. Even though chastity centers in the heart, it concerns the body, and either emotional desires or bodily senses can lead us away from it.

If you want to avoid impurity, don't touch, look at, listen to, or talk about impure things; as Paul puts it, impurity shouldn't even be mentioned among God's people (Eph. 5:3). Your hands, eyes, ears, and lips should all stay pure. According to Cassian, Basil one day remarked,

"I've never had sex, but I'm not a virgin." He meant, of course, that he had thought and spoken inappropriately. If you keep your mind on holy things, and delight in them, you will be purified.

# Chapter 13
*Spiritual Poverty*

Blessed are the poor in spirit, Matthew says (5:3), for theirs is the kingdom of heaven. Unhappy, then, are the rich in spirit, for theirs is the kingdom of hell. The rich in spirit I take to be those whose spirit is set on riches.

If you should happen to have riches, you should not have your heart filled with them; your heart should be like a buoy in the ocean—splashed over with waves, yet never permanently held in the depths. The buoy is always upright, pointed toward heaven, and impervious to the water trying to get in. Thus should your heart be; though riches may surround it, they never fill or overcome it.

Holding poison and being poisoned are two different things. A chemist may keep poisonous liquids on hand, but that doesn't mean he is being poisoned; they are in his lab, not his body. And you may have riches without being poisoned by them if you are merely using them and not focused on them.

Needless to say, this distinction is hard to put into practice. How many people in this world, whatever their financial condition, will admit to being greedy? When we desire more money, it's never "because we're greedy"—oh, no! It's because we want to have something to pass on to our children, or because we want to be prepared for this or that possible contingency. We never look around and say we have too much money. It's always the other way; we feel we need a little bit more. When we look for reasons why we need extra money, we always find them!

Moses saw a burning bush that stayed on fire without burning up. Greed is just the opposite; it consumes us spiritually without us realizing we're being eaten by its flames. Creating and satisfying material desires feels delightful!

Obviously, you need money for some things. But are you anxious about money? When there doesn't seem to be enough, do you long for some way to get more? We've all heard of gold fever, the willingness to leave behind everything and go anywhere in the hopes of striking it rich in a vein of ore; some people have such a money fever it's hard to imagine what they wouldn't do if the price were right.

Most of us are neither blindingly rich nor distressingly poor. Being in the middle class, with a mixture of money and needs, we have the difficult task of caring and not caring about money simultaneously. Even though money should mean less to us than to non-Christians, we should give more thought and care to how we spend it than they do.

How do you know whether you're too attached to things? Well, what happens when you lose some of them? If something that you own breaks and you get mad about it, you must have been pretty attached to that object. If you can't find something, and you're really upset about it, part of your heart must be wherever that object is.

To make sure you're not too attached to the things you own, practice "losing" them by giving some away. When people have fewer things than you do, give them some of yours. Do you truly love the poor? Then you'll want to share some of your possessions with them.

Paul says, "Who is weak, and I do not feel weak?" (2 Cor. 11:29 NIV). Love makes us share the feelings and circumstances of those we love. If we love poor people, we will share their poverty. You say you love the poor? Let's see if you have the signs. Do you spend time with poor people? Invite them to your house? Visit their homes? Talk with them? Sit by them in church? Take care of them when they're sick? Serving the poor is more glorious than sitting on a throne. And, in fact, the two things may be connected: Jesus, the King of the poor, the King of Kings, will say: "I was hungry and you gave me something to eat, I was thirsty and you gave me something to drink, I was a stranger and you invited me in, I needed clothes and you clothed me, I was sick and you looked after me, I was in prison and you came to visit me. . . . You who are blessed by my Father; take your inheritance, the kingdom prepared for you since the creation of the world" (Matt. 25:35–36, 34 NIV).

Actually, everybody has to experience poverty some time or other. Maybe a surprise guest will arrive and you don't have the house arranged the way you would like or you don't have fancy food ready to serve them. Maybe your luggage has gotten lost and you don't have nice clothes to wear on your trip. Maybe you've invited someone over for dinner but the food preparation has gone wrong and you can't serve what you had planned. This type of "temporary poverty" happens to everybody. Welcome these occasions! Bear with them cheerfully, and you are showing that your heart is not wrapped up in comfort.

Sometimes that temporary poverty becomes more serious. At some point in your life you may undergo a fire, flood, robbery, or lawsuit. At these crises, put on the patience that you have been practicing whenever small patches of temporary poverty have struck you.

# Chapter 14
*Friendship*

You should be helpful and nice to everyone, but with only a few people can you build a true and deep friendship. The best friendship comes from mutual support, emotionally and spiritually. For solid Christian friendship, share wisdom and insight; encourage each other in love, devotion, virtue, justice, self-control, and courage. In a real spiritual friendship, people share their spiritual goals and desires with each other, receiving back help and support in reaching those goals; this is what it means to be "one in spirit." Of course, some friendships will naturally be based on lesser things—those with neighbors, relatives, colleagues. But be sure to include in your life a few spiritual friendships, compared to which the others are only shadows.

Some writers may say that we shouldn't have any "special" friends—that we should try to treat everyone equally. Having a best friend, they argue, can contribute to jealousy and disunity. I think they're mistaken.

What kind of world do we live in? Making it through this life dedicated to God isn't like walking down a highway. It's more like struggling up a rough and slippery slope. If we were simply walking down a highway, we wouldn't need to help each other; but given the difficult path we have, we really need each other. With powerful, holy relationships, we have friends who can guide and help us through the most treacherous parts of life's journey.

Who do you think will help you when you're drawn by temptation, spiritually confused, or in despair? Your neighbors? Work colleagues? They may have different values and goals from yours. In times of spiritual crisis, Christians need close Christian friends to cling to. Even Jesus felt particular affection for John, Lazarus, Mary, and Martha.

Gregory Nazianzen, speaking of his friendship with Basil, said, "It seemed the two of us had but one soul, for we had the same aim: to practice virtue and center our lives on spiritual things, living in heaven while still part of the world."

As valuable as friendship is, I must warn you to be especially careful about one particular kind—spiritual friendships between men and women. When men and women see virtue in one another, it can often lead to them being in love with each other. They are first attracted to each other spiritually, but then other feelings enter in. One of the key danger signs is when a man and woman find that they start talking less about God and start talking more about each other, particularly praise of each other's personal characteristics. Falling in love is sort of like getting dizzy; we don't quite realize what is happening. In fact, one way to tell whether a friendship is good for us is this: A faulty friendship clouds our judgment, making us come up with excuses for poor behavior, whereas a holy friendship makes us clearsighted.

Let me say a word about what to do if you find yourself in an intersex friendship that seems to be taking a wrong turn, making you uncomfortable: Separate! If you can't separate altogether, eliminate all private meetings, secret talks, everything which indicates that the two of you have a "special" relationship. And, as another form of protection, let a wise and faithful friend know what's going on. If you do these things, God will protect you and keep your friendships pure and holy.

# Chapter 15
*The Heart*

Some people say that, to change a person, start with trying to change their appearance or manners. On the contrary, I think we have to start with the heart. God says, "Return to me with all your heart" (Joel 2:12 NIV) and "My son, give me your heart" (Prov. 23:26 NIV). Our actions take shape from the form of our hearts. Whoever has Christ in his heart has Christ in everything he does. Just like an oak tree grows from an acorn, I want your life to grow out of Jesus in your heart. Thus it is that Paul can say, "I no longer live, but Christ lives in me" (Gal. 2:20 NIV). So gaining the heart for Christ is most important. Yet outward actions do have some effect on us.

Take fasting, for instance. It maintains our mastery over gluttony and puts the fear of God into the devil. Frequent fasting is not as necessary as simply showing that we *can* fast when it seems important.

I'm not talking about long, hard fasting, by the way; a stag can't run when it's fat, but it can't run when it's half-starved, either. We need moderation in everything, including spiritual disciplines. If you mistreat your body when you're young, you may have to pamper it when you're old. It's much better to be reasonable throughout your whole life.

You can maintain control of your body in two ways: by fasting and by working. I would rather you worked a lot than fasted a lot; working accomplishes more. One per-son fasts; another person serves the sick, visits shut-ins, preaches, helps people in need, etc. All those activities are more valuable than fasting. In general, it's better to strengthen our bodies for service than to weaken them.

Remember what Jesus said to the disciples: "Eat what is set before you" (Luke 10:8 NIV). In my opinion, this is quite a virtue, to eat what's set in front of us, to adjust our taste buds to it, and not to complain about how anything is cooked.

Now obviously I'm not talking about eating food that's bad for you. If it's too rich for you, or it gives you gas, then leave it alone! Moderation is the key to healthy eating— none of these starvation diets that end in eating like a pig.

Consider the story of Balaam from the Book of Numbers. Balaam, you may recall, was disobeying the Lord on a trip. Since his heart was not right, an angel with a sword stood in the pathway to kill him. The ass Balaam was riding saw this angel and swerved aside. Balaam beat the ass with his staff. In a miracle, God gave the ass the ability to speak, and it said, "Why are you doing this to me?"

Balaam answered, "You're making a fool out of me."

Then the angel appeared to Balaam's sight and said, "I've been here in the path waiting to take your life." Notice, in this story, that Balaam was the one at fault but the ass got the beating.

How often, when our hearts are wrong, we damage our bodies with worry and anger and gluttony and fear. If our bodies could speak to us like the ass did to Balaam, they would say, "What are you hurting me for? Why are you bringing these backaches and headaches and stomachaches onto me? And why are you blaming me for them? Have good thoughts and I'll stay out of trouble.

You throw me into a fire and get mad at me for burning; you throw smoke in my eyes and get mad when it's hard to see." To conclude, spiritual discipline is indeed useful, but most useful of all is to have a devoted heart.

## Chapter 16
*Being With Others, Being Alone*

We Christians are supposed to love our neighbors as ourselves. If you try to avoid spending time with other people, how can you think you love them? If you can't be content with spending time alone, do you properly love yourself?

When you're with other people, be a Christian, but be a relaxed one. Some people are so tense about saying and doing what "religious people are supposed to" that they're downright annoying. It's like taking a walk with somebody who counts all the steps out loud! When you're with others, rejoice in the Lord.

By the way, I don't count making fun of people when they do something stupid as part of "rejoicing in the Lord." Some good-natured laughter at a minor predicament, on the other hand, can provide innocent amusement. The difference is whether you're merely enjoying the oddity of the situation or whether there's a bit of "putting someone else down" involved. Now when it comes to wit and wordplay—those are always welcome! One time at a social gathering when some people tried to talk with a devout king about some very serious topic, he said, "Right now's not a good time for that; anybody heard a good joke lately?"

Be sincere and honest with people; never tell a lie. Our God is a God of truth (Ps. 31:5). But keep in mind that being truthful doesn't have to mean telling everything you know! If you accidentally say something false, correct it as soon as possible.

Try to make your words match what you mean; if you're hungry, don't say "I'm starving." In the *Confessions,* Augustine said that when his best friend died he felt half dead himself and didn't even want to live anymore. Later, in the *Retractions,* he took it back, saying that he had exaggerated to try to show people what a loving friend he was.

Do you want to avoid arguments? Louis of France said one way to do this is simply not to contradict what other people say, unless agreeing with them would be sinful or harmful. When we do have to contradict people, we should try to do so tactfully; you don't get ahead spiritually or socially by being a know-it-all! When there's a conversation going on, contribute to it; that shows you like engaging the minds of the people you're with. But always remember the difference between contributing to conversation and dominating it!

Spend time with yourself as well—read a Christian book, think about God, think about ultimate things in general. A famous bishop, Gregory Nazianzen, writes, "I like walking on the beach by myself at sunset; it helps me toss off some of my daily troubles." Even Jesus said to the disciples, "Come with me by yourselves to a quiet place and get some rest" (Mark 6:31 NIV).

You need some recreation to relax the mind and body. Why doesn't a hunter always keep his bowstring pulled back? It would wear out both his arm and the string, making him a less effective hunter. Similarly, some time away from our usual routine can enable us to concentrate better when we return. Don't be so strict with yourself (and with others!) as to leave out recreation. Go out for some fresh air, have a friendly conversation, sing, play a musical instrument.

Play games—tennis, basketball, chess, board games—anything like that is good if you don't overdo it. If you spend too much time playing games, it's not a recreation; it's an occupation! Five or six hours of tennis will wear you out rather than refreshing you, and so (mentally) will five or six hours of chess. Also, don't get involved in playing games for high stakes; that's not a reasonable way to live, and players tend to get too emotionally involved. The general principle is to enjoy playing games (if you didn't, they wouldn't be recreation), but not to get so wrapped up in them that you feel deprived if you have to go a few days without your "fun time."

## Chapter 17
*Judgmentalism*

Jesus said, "Do not judge, and you will not be judged. Do not condemn, and you will not be condemned" (Luke 6:37 NIV). Paul added, "Therefore judge nothing before the appointed time; wait till the Lord comes. He will bring to light what is hidden in darkness and expose the motives of men's hearts" (1 Cor. 4:5 NIV). It's foolish to judge others because, to a great extent, the evil of an action depends on the intention of the actor, and that's hidden inside a person's heart; how are we going to know what it is? We have enough to keep us busy just with judging ourselves; as Paul says, "If we judged ourselves, we would not come under judgment" (1 Cor. 11:31 NIV). But we tend to do just the opposite; we don't judge ourselves, but we judge the people around us every chance we get.

Some people judge because they have a naturally harsh personality. That's perhaps an imperfection rather than a sin, but it leads to the sin of judgmentalism. These folks need to go to a spiritual "doctor" and say, "Can you give me a prescription for becoming a gentler person?"

Other people judge inappropriately out of pride; by lowering others, they feel they are raising themselves. "I am not like other men" the foolish Pharisee said (Luke 18:11 NIV). This causes some of us pleasure; by noting the imperfections of others, we congratulate ourselves on being above average in morality. This smug and subtle self-satisfaction is enormously hard to detect, by the way; we usually aren't aware we feel this way unless somebody points it out.

Some of us like to assume the worst of others, because then we don't feel so bad about being sinful ourselves. If the church seems full of "sinners," then we're just one of the crowd; there's strength in numbers! And finally, many of us engage in a "halo and horns" effect; if we like somebody, we tend to gloss over their faults, but if we dislike somebody, we go out of our way to put the worst possible construction on everything they say and do.

What's the remedy for all this judgmentalism? Charity, plain and simple. The more loving we are in general, the gentler our judgments will be.

Let me give you an example. When Isaac went to the land of the Philistines (Gen. 26), he was afraid they would kill him to get his wife Rebecca, because she was so exceptionally beautiful. So Isaac told everyone Rebecca was his sister. King Abimelech one day happened to catch Isaac caressing Rebecca in a sexual manner and said to him, "She is really your wife!" (Gen. 26:9 NIV). An evil-minded man might have assumed Isaac was committing incest, or that Rebecca was a prostitute of some sort instead of Isaac's wife. But Abimelech instantly put the most charitable construction to his accusation. If someone appears to be engaging in questionable behavior, and there are a hundred different ways to explain what they're doing, we should automatically incline toward the most positive one.

In the New Testament, Joseph discovered that Mary was pregnant, and he knew he hadn't caused it. There appeared to be only one possible explanation! Yet, in spite of the fact that there was really only one choice (it seemed), Joseph took Mary's purity and holiness into account and figured that somehow she must be less guilty than things appeared. In spite of the fact that he could have created an uproar, he decided to end things quietly. The Bible says Joseph "did not want to expose her to public disgrace" because he was "a righteous man" (Matt. 1:19 NIV).

A final example. Jesus was on the cross, and clearly the people that put Him there were guilty of sin. Yet what does He say? "Father, forgive them, for they do not know what they are doing" (Luke 23:34 NIV). Guilty as they were, Christ was looking for a way to minimize their evil, and He publicly acknowledged that they did not realize the enormity of their crime. If someone is clearly engaging in sin, and we have to recognize it, at least let us be like Jesus by considering the possibility of background or personality difficulty or ignorance of consequences in contributing to it.

So are we never to judge others? That's right—never. But immediately I must explain what I mean by judgment. To "judge others" in the Christian sense means to be judgmental—to let our negative feelings come into play as we determine whether someone is guilty and their level of culpability. You see, when a judge sentences someone in a courtroom, he is not being judgmental. He is actually acting on behalf of God, delivering the sentence of society that a person has acted in a wrong way. But if a judge lets his feelings get involved, and adds to the sentence from personal distaste or expresses the sentence in a harsh way, then he is no longer acting as a representative of God to keep order in society but is instead judging in the unchristian sense.

To see or know something is not to judge; and to doubt or suspect (when there is reason for doing so) is not being judgmental. To sum it all up, we probably won't have as many problems with being judgmental if we primarily concern ourselves with our own behavior. Of course, sometimes duty requires us to concern ourselves with the behavior of others—if we head a household, for instance, or hold a community position such as teaching or a church position such as pastoring. So the general rule is, do your duty, and otherwise mind your own business. . . .

# Chapter 18
## *Talking About Others*

Perhaps the worst thing about judgmentalism is that it leads us to talk about other people in a negative way. In Isaiah 6, an angel took a burning coal from a heavenly altar and touched it to Isaiah's lips to purify his speech. If I could take just one coal from that altar, I'd like to take the one that would purify people from gossip! Saying bad things about other people, you're sooner or later going to say a bad thing that's wrong or exaggerated, and then you've stolen your victim's good name. How can a thief make it to heaven? Do you want to show up at the pearly gates with somebody's good name on your hands?

Slander is murder. We each have three lives: our spiritual life, which depends on the grace of God, can be destroyed by sin; our physical life, which depends on having the soul inside, can be destroyed by death; and our social life, which depends on our reputation, can be destroyed by gossip. Anybody who slanderously gossips is (figuratively) committing a murder/suicide: They're killing someone else's reputation and their own spiritual life.

Bernard put it this way: "Evil gossip is a form of demon possession; the speaker has a devil controlling his tongue, and the eager hearer has a devil controlling his ear."

Reader, I am pleading with you not to engage in this type of behavior. Here are some things to avoid:

* Don't say that others are evil when there's still doubt about their guilt.
* Don't make known people's evil deeds that are secret.
* Don't exaggerate evil deeds that are known.
* Don't put a bad construction on a possibly innocent action.

People who start out by saying something positive are the worst of all. "He sure is a great guy," they say, "and I really like him, but did you know that he. . ." "Everybody thinks the world of her," they remark, "and you probably do, too, but there's one thing I think you ought to know about her: she. . ." It's like an archer pulling a bow as far back as possible; these people seem at first to be on the victim's side, so when the evil words eventually come, they fly out with greater force and get driven more deeply into the hearers' hearts.

Don't call a person a drunk because you saw her have too much to drink once; don't call a person a liar because you once caught him in a lie. A person does not merit a label from a fault on a single occasion. After all, the sky turned dark the day Christ died, but we do not therefore call 3:00 P.M. the middle of the night! For someone to deserve a label (whether good or bad), their actions in that area must be habitual.

Actually, it's dangerous to give labels at any time, because people can and do change. God gives grace freely and instantaneously, so how do you know the "big sinner" of yesterday is the big sinner of today? You can't judge today by yesterday; only at the end of time are judgments irrevocable. You can't label a living person wicked without taking a chance on being wrong; the safer thing to say is that he did whatever evil thing last week, or that he was engaged in a certain evil activity for several years. You can't automatically argue from the past to the present, and definitely not from the past to the future.

Don't get me wrong here. I'm not saying that, to protect people, we should call bad things good. If a person slanders, don't speak of it as a positive thing by saying, "Well, at least she says what she thinks." If someone has an affair, don't say, "Well, it's good he's letting his wife know his needs."

To sum up, choose your words carefully. If a man and woman seem to you to be moving into a danger area relationally, and you are discussing it with someone (say, to wonder whether you should bring it up to the couple), don't imply more than you know; simply describe the situation and ask whether it should call for action or silence on your part. When you are speaking about an acquaintance, your tongue is sharp as a surgeon's knife; you have to be extremely careful to avoid damage.

## Chapter 19
### *Being Faithful and Reasonable*

Our sacred Spouse wants us to love Him in both great things and small. We should be ready to sacrifice whatever God requires: father, mother, sibling, sight, life itself. But God doesn't usually ask for these types of abandonings; more often He asks us to show our love during small trials, minor inconveniences, little everyday annoyances of life. How can you really show your love for God? By expressing that love while undergoing a head-ache, a toothache, a cold, an irritable spouse, a whiny colleague, a broken glass, a lost set of keys, a job at church that you're not particularly eager to do.

One of God's great saints was a woman of Siena named Catherine. She was obviously deeply devout; I read of her spiritual raptures and wise counsel with awe. But here's what's equally impressive: In her parents' house she kept the fire going, roasted the meat, kneaded and baked the bread—well, she really did just about everything necessary to keep the household going. She wrote that when cooking for her parents, she would imagine she was Martha doing it for Jesus.

Prayer and meditation and communion perhaps raise us as high toward heaven as we can get in this life. But while continuing in those great and important things, don't forget to cultivate humbler virtues—visiting the sick, helping the poor, taking care of your family's needs. It's like growing flowers at the foot of the cross.

Having the chance to teach a crowd of 5000, like Jesus did, is pretty rare; but everybody gets chances to be faithful in little things. So do everything in Jesus' name—eating or drinking (as in Col. 3:17), playing tennis, broiling a chicken—this is what it means to do the will of God.

Most of us think of ourselves as reasonable human beings; most of us are wrong. Self-love continually diverts us away from reason and into small (but significant) unjust, unfair ways of thinking. Consider the following common ways that people think, and determine whether thoroughly reasonable creatures would hold these ideas:

* When we do selfish or improper things, we make excuses; when other people do similar things, we condemn them.
* We want to sell high (very high) but be able to buy cheap (very cheap).
* We want to see justice done, except when we are at fault; then we prefer mercy.
* We get irritated when people tease us; but when we make fun of them, we think they ought to realize that "it's only a joke."
* When others disagree with us over a particular political or social issue, which they have a right to do, we find ourselves irritated with them.
* We shower approval on attractive people, and want to be around them more, even though there's really no correlation between appearance and goodness.
* We want people to be instantly and humbly

       grateful when we point out their faults, even
       though that's not our own initial reaction.

\*   If we are involved with four others in a pro-
       ject, all five of us feel we are doing at least
       our share, and most of us think we are doing
       more!

Proverbs 20:23 (NIV) says, "The Lord detests differing weights, and dishonest scales do not please him." Well, most of us don't have a problem with this verse literally, but don't we weigh our actions on a different scale from the actions of others? One could almost say we have two hearts: a nice, soft, friendly heart for ourselves, and a rough, tough, strict heart for others.

Be fair—emotionally and materially. When you're selling something, imagine if you were buying it what you'd want to pay; when you're buying, imagine what you'd want to get for it if you were selling. This exercise will keep you from trying to rip people off.

We need to be reasonable in our desires as well. A lot of people waste time daydreaming about things that can't (or shouldn't) happen. What good does it do for a married woman to daydream about being single again? Or about being married to someone else? I can easily see, however, the harm it can do. When you hear someone with a beautiful voice sing in church, what good does it do (if you can't sing) to daydream about yourself singing in church like that? If you want to imagine something, imagine what God can do with the abilities that you have now! Some people daydream about what great things they could do for God in the jungles of Africa, and then they go outside and gripe about what a hot day it is! A reasonable Christian's greatest desire will be to grow in love for God where she is.

# Chapter 20
## *Marriage*

Jesus got invited to a wedding in Cana of Galilee, and I wish He got invited to more weddings today. I'm afraid most contemporary couples want Venus at their weddings more than they want Jesus! Your wedding ceremony and festivities make a statement about what you want your marriage to be.

Everybody always says couples should only get married if they love each other, but that word isn't clear enough in our society; we need to specify what type of love we're talking about. Marital love needs to be the kind Paul recommended: "Husbands, love your wives, just as Christ loved the church" (Eph. 5:25 NIV). And you wives need to love your husbands as the church loves Christ. Adam and Eve were given to each other by God, and you married couples should consider yourselves given to each other by God.

Husbands, keep a constant and heartfelt love for your wives. Any weakness they display, whether physical or spiritual, should not lead you to look down on them but should instead move you to compassion. "Husbands," Peter says, "in the same way be considerate as you live with your wives, and treat them with respect as the weaker partner" (1 Pet. 3:7 NIV). Wives, love your husbands with affectionate respect; God has created them as the more vigorous sex, even showing by the creation process that woman depends on man.

Gregory Nazianzen wrote that in his day couples used to celebrate the anniversary of the day they got married, and I'd like to see this custom revived. The celebration should include some sort of joyous celebration, such as a nice meal together, and some sort of spiritual renewing, such as taking communion together. The couple should pray together, renewing their commitment to each other, asking God to help them keep that commitment and to bless their relationship in every way.

The marriage bed should be kept pure, Hebrews tells us (13:4); to comment on this, I would like to draw some analogies between eating and sex, as both involve physical appetites.

1. Eating was set up by God to keep people alive. This means the act of eating is in itself a good thing, a thing that honors God because it fulfills His purposes. And as sex was ordained by God to keep the human race alive, it is in itself a good thing.

2. But eating does more than simply preserve life. When we eat together with people, we relax with them and enjoy their company, and sex provides this for husbands and wives. In 1 Corinthians 7, Paul calls the sexual satisfying of one's spouse a "debt," a debt that he won't even allow to be halted for "spiritual" reasons (except briefly by mutual consent). If providing sexual satisfaction is that important, how much worse is it to deprive a spouse because of anger or irritation.

3. When we eat with others we should indicate that we are enjoying the food and the experience of eating with them; the same is true of sex!

4. To act like a glutton turns eating from a holy act into a bad thing, whether it comes from eating too much or too often or in a disgusting way. Similarly, we can ruin sex by being gluttonous or pushy with our mates.

This is sort of an uncomfortable subject for me to cover, as a single man, so I'll stop here; I think I've covered the main things that need to be said.

# Chapter 21
*Fighting Temptation*

I magine a young princess, deeply loved by her husband. Now imagine some evil man who, wanting to have sex with her, sends a messenger to her telling of his desires. What are the steps involved? First, the messenger tells the princess about the temptation; second, she decides whether she likes the idea or not; third, she decides whether to agree or not.

We, of course, are the princess, deeply loved by Christ, and sin comes to us the same way. First, Satan brings the idea of the sin to our minds; second, we either like the idea or we don't; third, we decide whether to go along or not. These three steps of sin—temptation, pleasure, consent—are not always easy to distinguish, but they always occur in some form.

Temptation, no matter how long it lasts, cannot harm us spiritually as long as we don't enjoy it or give in to it. In fact, feeling distressed by tempting desires is a positive sign, showing that we don't want to take pleasure in considering them. One way the princess analogy I used above breaks down is that the princess could always get rid of the messenger, whereas we may have to struggle with certain temptations for years. But temptation that we don't like can never hurt us.

What if we do like the temptation? There's an interesting story about the woman from Siena, Catherine, that I have mentioned earlier. She wanted to be sexually pure, but her mind kept filling with thoughts of men and women having sex and telling her what she was missing. Even while her will rejected the temptation, her heart kept finding pleasure and excitement in thinking about it; she was simultaneously attracted and repelled.

After struggling with these thoughts for years, one day she was praying and seemed to have a sort of conversation with Jesus. "Lord, where have You been while my heart has been filled with these impure pleasures?" she asked.

"I've been in your heart, daughter," He seemed to say.

"How could You possibly be living in my heart when it was so unclean?"

"Tell me something," Jesus asked. "Were you happy about having those impure thoughts, or were you upset?"

"I was tremendously upset," Catherine answered.

"Who do you think caused that distress?" Jesus said. "If your heart had been all alone, you would have only had pleasure in those thoughts. But I was hidden deeply there, and though you did not have the purity not to take pleasure in the thoughts, I enabled you to have the strength not to yield to them. Your resistance, with My support, of something that seemed enticing has actually made you a stronger person."

We can see from this that even when a person is tempted, and wants to give in, the refusal of consent can still honor God. But don't get confident about your ability to withstand temptation; it's only by God's grace that anyone overcomes.

To return to the princess illustration: She was not blamable for the temptation because it was made without her permission. But suppose she had encouraged this man to send her a note of love. Then, even if she refused to have sex with him, she is still at fault for encouraging the proposition.

Undergoing temptation is blamable if we deliberately bring the temptation on ourselves. For example, suppose I know that every time I play a certain game I lose my temper; it's wrong for me to keep playing that game. If I know that every time I hang around with a certain friend we wind up drinking too much, it's wrong for me to hang around with that friend.

When you find yourself tempted, follow the example of a little child who sees a ferocious-looking dog; immediately he turns to his parents for help. As soon as you recognize you're in a tempting situation, turn immediately to God in prayer. Don't focus on the temptation; focus on God.

If you were faced with a wolf, you would instantly recognize you were in danger; but with a fly or mosquito you would not be so alarmed, even though insects can carry major diseases. In the same way, it's easy to keep from murdering; we know that would harm our spiritual well-being. But it's hard to keep from expressing irritation. Similarly, it's:

> EASY. . .to keep from having an affair.
> HARD. . .to keep from flirting.
> EASY. . .to preserve your body for your spouse alone.
> HARD. . .to preserve your heart for your spouse alone.
> EASY. . .to avoid stealing from a store.
> HARD. . .to avoid stealing from an office.
> EASY. . .to avoid perjury in a court.
> HARD. . .to avoid casual lying.
> EASY. . .not to wish an enemy's death.
> HARD. . .not to wish him a bad break of some kind.
> EASY. . .not to get drunk.
> HARD. . .not to overeat.

As you can see, the majority of our spiritual life involves dealing with "little" temptations.

# Chapter 22
*Depression and Anxiety*

One of the great problems with depression is that when we try to fight against it and fail, that leaves us more depressed. We are thereby weakened for our next bout against it, and the cycle continues.

Depression is often brought on by anxiety. Where does anxiety come from? It occurs because (1) we are undergoing something bad that we want to end, but we don't know when and whether it will, or (2) there's something good we really want, but we don't know whether we'll be able to get it or not.

What's the best way to escape anxiety? It's not to focus on escaping the evil situation or attaining the good. When a child has a knot in a shoelace, as he gets more frustrated, one of the things he does is pull harder and harder on the end of the string. That just pulls the knot tighter and tighter! What we need to do first, instead of "pulling" violently at the situation, is to pursue spiritual peace and quiet. Then, once your mind and spirit are under God's control, you can gently pursue your goal. "Gently" doesn't mean carelessly, but it means without feeling pressured.

Examine yourself once a day to see whether your

heart is still under God's control or whether it has been "captured" by a particular worry or fear. If your heart's been taken away, capture it back and present it to God your King once again. If you're upset about something, determine not to engage the situation until you've first asked God to ease your upset feelings.

Regarding sadness in general, Paul says that "Godly sorrow brings repentance that leads to salvation and leaves no regret, but worldly sorrow leaves death" (2 Cor. 7:10 NIV). So clearly sorrow can be either good or bad, depending on what it brings about.

Just as Satan wants wicked people to feel comfortable in their sins, he wants good people to feel depressed in their virtue. Just as Satan tempts people to evil by making it look appealing, he tempts people away from good by making it seem unappealing. He wants us to be depressed and despairing for all eternity because that's the way he is, and misery loves company!

Depression saps people's energy and makes it hard for us to formulate and work toward goals. Depression is like a hard winter that kills the plants and freezes the earth, for it kills our drive to achieve and leaves us feeling paralyzed. What should you do when suffering from depression? For one thing, I suggest praying to and speaking to God (both mentally and vocally) with phrases that remind you of His goodness and power: "God, You are my joy and hope." "You are my loving Savior." "You are my true Spouse." And use Biblical phrases that inspire confidence in God, such as "Who shall separate us from the love of Christ?" (Rom. 8:35 NIV).

Also, sing spiritual songs. Remember how music drove away the evil spirit that depressed King Saul.

Keep busy with a variety of activities and occupy your mind to keep it from continually mulling over whatever troubles you.

Philosophically, consider what kind of world we live in. The world has existed for ages, yet it continually changes: Day turns to night, spring to summer, fall to winter. Even in the same season, no two days are exactly alike: each will be a little rainier, windier, drier, sunnier, cooler, warmer, or cloudier than the ones before and after. This continual changing gives people something interesting to talk about! Humanity has sometimes been called a miniature world, and in ourselves we see the same level of changing: Sometimes we get scared, sometimes hopeful, sometimes excited, sometimes irritated. No day is exactly like the next.

Keep this in mind, because our goal should be to preserve spiritual commitment amidst a whirl of changing circumstances and feelings; even if every person and every event around us alters, our eyes and hearts are to stay fixed on God. A ship out on the ocean may be headed north, south, east, or west, but its compass will always point to the North Star. Even when our world seems turned upside down, whether we're undergoing sorrow or joy, comfort or pain, pleasure or boredom, God is always the same. Absolutely nothing can separate us from His love. And since that love is more powerful than the ups and downs of the world, if we hold on to it we'll be able to keep our spiritual balance.

# Chapter 23
*Keeping the Devout Life Going*

Being a committed Christian is hard. We're frail beings, and without continual movement toward renewal we're going to plummet to the ground, spiritually speaking. No matter how good a car is, it needs the oil changed from time to time, the spark plugs tuned up, and worn-out engine and body parts replaced. Our hearts need, at the very least, an annual spiritual tune-up to keep us running smoothly for God.

Just as fresh oil keeps a car engine running smoothly, we should keep our hearts running smoothly with confession and communion. Gregory Nazianzen says the early Christians used to use a baptism anniversary to renew their vows to God, and that's not a bad idea. Here are some things you might say:

"God, I have determined to forsake and detest sin forever. I consecrate my body and heart and mind to loving You. When I live for You, I am clearly a better person than when I live for myself. You have saved me from death; being united to You is being united to the very source of life. Thank You, God. Please fill me with good desires and help me to make this year a powerful one spiritually."

Remember that you don't have to kneel to pray. You

can do it walking along or even lying in bed, if you're awake enough.

One thing you might examine from time to time is your attitude toward God. Consider some of these things:

1. How do you feel about God's commandments? Do you find them good and uplifting?
2. How do you feel about spiritual exercises? Do you find the following activities enjoyable or repulsive:
   * Reading and talking about the Bible?
   * Praying?
   * Confessing?
   * Setting up spiritual goals and plans?
   * Receiving spiritual advice?
   * Taking communion?
3. How do you feel about God Himself? Do you like Him? Do you say nice things about Him to people? Do you ever do anything you don't particularly want to just because you think it will make God happy?

A further thing to reflect upon is your attitude toward yourself. Consider some of these questions:

1. Are you ready to leave this world whenever it pleases God?
2. Does your life have a guiding principle? Does it make sense?
3. How much do you really care for yourself spiritually?
4. What do your chief fears and desires say about you?
5. How do you talk about yourself? Are you humble or do you want attention?
6. Do you repeatedly engage in pleasures that aren't in your own best interest? To give one example, do you keep yourself from getting enough sleep?

# Chapter 24
*Final Considerations*

O ne characteristic of the devout Christian is, from time to time, simply thinking through some things that most people seldom consider. To get the maximum benefit from the following items for reflection, begin by recognizing that you are in God's presence, and ask Him to give you the grace to yield yourself more fully to His love and service. Here are some spiritually useful topics:

1. Think about your soul's reasoning ability, the fact that you can understand things. You can comprehend, for instance, that there is a God, that He is powerful, that He is good. You can understand the idea of forever and logically reason that the choices we make in this world will likely affect our future life.
2. Think about the sort of heart you have. Nothing on this earth seems to satisfy it permanently. You've been around long enough to know that good things don't last. Our heart has desires, so we try to satisfy them by pursuing created things, but even when we get them the pleasure of achievement fades away.

3. Think about how much more admirable virtue is than vice. Which of the following characteristics do people (including yourself) respect and appreciate more:
   * Patience or revenge?
   * Gentleness or irritability?
   * Humility or pride?
   * Generosity or stinginess?
   * Temperance or addiction?

   People like each other, and even themselves, better when the right spiritual choices are made. This is a kind of pleasure you can feel free to strive for!

4. Think about Christ's love, especially that it has been given to you. Christ's sacrifice gives you various types of grace—grace to want to follow Him, grace to keep trying to grow, and grace to succeed in growth! Even though God loves so many people, He still loves you as fully as He can love, just like the sun can shine brightly a thousand places on earth and still have just as much light left for the place where you live. He "loved me and gave himself for me" (Gal. 2:20 NIV) Paul says, speaking of Christ; Paul makes it sound as though Christ did this for him personally! Similarly, apply these thoughts to yourself.

5. Finally, think about how long God has loved you. When did He start? When you were born? No, because His love is eternal. "I have loved you with an everlasting love," God tells His people (Jer. 31:3 NIV). God's love for you has no beginning nor end.

To make sure your thoughts affect your life, take practical steps to ensure growth takes place: prayer, communion, good deeds, avoiding occasions that lead to sin, practicing the counsel of wise advisors, and so forth. On a regular basis, commit yourself orally to obeying God, no matter what.

Make statements aloud regarding the continual renewing of your life. Consider saying one of these:

* I am not my own; I belong to my Savior.
* I have nothing of my own; everything belongs to Jesus.
* The world can't tell I've changed, but I really have, because the change is happening in my heart.

Some people might say, my dear friend, that if you really tried to live for God you wouldn't have time for anything else! That's nonsense. True, there are a lot of spiritual disciplines; but the choice of which ones to focus on at any given time will vary with each life situation. Think about how many laws your country has; you're supposed to obey them all, but a lot of them don't even apply to you, and even the ones that do apply don't necessarily affect your life on a daily basis. So make an effort to engage in spiritual devotion, and God will give you the time and energy for it, even if He has to make the sun stand still like He did for Joshua! Things get done when God works with us.

The other objection people might have is that it takes somebody really "religious" or "superspiritual" to lead a consecrated life. Well, over the years I have noticed that people who really want to lead Christ-centered lives, and who ask wise Christians for advice on how to do it, wind up achieving it.

Finally, someone might say that it shouldn't have to take a book like this for someone to be able to live the Christian life. To this you can humbly answer, "That's true.

But it takes books like this for *me* to be able to live the Christian life."

When living the Christian life seems hard, remember the little poem of St. Francis of Assisi:

When life seems hard and labors long,
I think of heaven—and find I'm strong.

May Jesus rule! To Him, and the Father, and the Holy Spirit, be honor and glory both now and forevermore. Amen.

# THE
# ESSENTIAL CHRISTIAN LIBRARY

*Books That Stand the Test of Time. . .
Priced as if Time Were Standing Still*

Essential reading for every Christian, these hardbound, time-tested classics will form a priceless collection of Christian writing that will bring inspiration and encourage devotion to God for years to come. Beautifully bound, affordably priced at $9.97 each!

*Best of Andrew Murray on Prayer, The*
*Christian's Secret of A Happy Life, The* by Hannah Whitall Smith
*Faith's Great Heroes, Volume One*
*Great Sermons, Volume One*
*God Calling* edited by A.J. Russell
*Hiding Place, The* by Corrie ten Boom
*Hinds' Feet On High Places* by Hannah Hurnard
*In His Steps* by Charles M. Sheldon
*Morning & Evening* by Charles H. Spurgeon
*My Utmost for His Highest* by Oswald Chambers
*Pilgrim's Progress, The* by John Bunyan
*Prison to Praise* by Merlin Carothers
*Riches of Bunyan, The*

Available wherever books are sold.
Or order from:

Barbour Publishing, Inc.
P.O. Box 719
Uhrichsville, OH 44683
http://www.barbourbooks.com

If you order by mail add $2.00 to your order for shipping.
Prices subject to change without notice.

ISBN 1-57748-446-0

9 781577 484462

90000